CAMBRIDGE LIBRARY COLLECTION

Books of enduring scholarly value

African Studies

This series focuses on Africa during the period of European colonial expansion. It includes anthropological studies, travel accounts from missionaries and explorers (including those searching for the sources of the Nile and the Congo), and works that shed light on colonial concerns such as gold mining, big game hunting, trade, education and political rivalries.

A Report of the Kingdom of Congo and of the Surrounding Countries

In this 1591 work, mathematician Filippo Pigafetta (1533–1604) explains that he was ordered by Pope Sixtus V to transcribe the account of Duarte Lopez, a Portuguese who had spent twelve years in the Congo. Lopez had hoped that the pope would give him support in his mission to the Congolese, but this was not forthcoming: he returned to Africa, and was not heard from again. The work was first translated into English by the English antiquary Abraham Hartwell: this translation with notes by Margarite Hutchinson was published in 1881. (It has not been possible to reissue the accompanying map.) Lopez's narrative gives a detailed account of his voyage on his uncle's ship and the history and geography of the kingdom and its six administrative regions under the rule of its king (named by Lopez 'Don Alvarez'). This fascinating account demonstrates the extent of Portuguese exploration across West Africa in the sixteenth century, of which later explorers were unaware.

T0370909

A Report of the Kingdom of Congo and of the Surrounding Countries

Drawn out of the Writings and Discourses of the Portuguese, Duarte Lopez, by Filippo Pigafetta, in Rome, 1591

Duarte Lopez
Filippo Pigafetta
Margarite Hutchinson
Thomas Fowell Buxton

Cambridge University Press

CAMBRIDGE
UNIVERSITY PRESS

University Printing House, Cambridge, CB2 8BS, United Kingdom

Cambridge University Press is part of the University of Cambridge.
It furthers the University's mission by disseminating knowledge in the pursuit of education, learning and research at the highest international levels of excellence.

www.cambridge.org
Information on this title: www.cambridge.org/9781108082747

This edition first published 1881
This digitally printed version 2018

ISBN 978-1-108-08274-7 Paperback

A REPORT

OF THE

KINGDOM OF CONGO.

LONDON :
GILBERT AND RIVINGTON, PRINTERS,
ST. JOHN'S SQUARE.

A REPORT

OF THE

KINGDOM OF CONGO,

AND OF THE

Surrounding Countries;

Drawn out of the Writings and Difcourfes of the Portuguefe,

DUARTE LOPEZ,

BY FILIPPO PIGAFETTA, IN ROME, 1591.

Newly Translated from the Italian, and Edited, with Explanatory Notes,

BY

MARGARITE HUTCHINSON.

With Facsimiles of the Original Maps, and a Preface by

SIR THOMAS FOWELL BUXTON, BART., F.R.G.S.,

ETC., ETC.

"There lies the Congo Kingdom, great and ftrong,
Already led by us to Chriftian ways;
Where flows Zaire, the river clear and long,
A ftream unfeen by men of olden days."

The Lusiads, v. 13.

LONDON:
JOHN MURRAY, ALBEMARLE STREET.
1881.

CONTENTS.

BOOK THE FIRST.

BOOK THE SECOND.

PREFACE.

THE laſt twenty-five years have ſeen the veil drawn back from a great part of the continent of Africa. The labours of many travellers following in the ſteps of Livingſtone have combined to throw a light on the Dark Continent, of which we knew as little as the inhabitants knew of us. We have learnt much of the phyſical features of the country, and of the character of the tribes with whom explorers have made acquaintance, but we have alſo learnt that much that has appeared to us ſo new was, in fact, only rediſcovered.

The maps of the 16th century fairly illuſtrate the knowledge of that time. If we compare them with the maps of the beginning of the 19th century, we cannot fail to obſerve how much of that knowledge was loſt, although more recent explorations ſhowed how much of truth was contained in them.

The tranſlation that is now offered to the public will have its uſe in ſhowing the kind of information that was to be had in Europe in the 16th century, and the character of the men who obtained it.

It may do more. It may ſtimulate reſearch into this long-neglected portion of hiſtory; and poſſibly the inveſtigation of libraries in Portugal and Spain may yet throw more light on the condition of Central Africa at that time, and on the nature of the Portugueſe Government over it; and, perhaps, give us ſome anſwer to the queſtions how that government was formed, and how it came to be loſt. Such queſtions could not fail to be of intereſt to any nation that poſſeſſes or has poſſeſſed authority in Africa. It would be information full of intereſt to us if it enabled us to know by what ſteps the authority was gained—whether in conſequence of the deliberate intention of the Government at Liſbon, or by the efforts of Portugueſe ſettled in the interior. Again, it was loſt—utterly forgotten—leaving no traces behind it, unleſs the Indian corn and the tobacco plants are such. We should gladly welcome any information that ſhowed whether the reins of government were drawn too tight, till they broke, or whether they fell from the hands of rulers who ruled without diligence.

The accounts of the travels of Pigafetta, as narrated by Duarte Lopez, give a valuable inſight into the knowledge then exiſting in Europe. They alſo ſupply a further illuſtration of the activity then diſplayed by the Courts at Rome and Liſbon in ſending out miſſionary expeditions to Africa; but they tell us nothing to explain how it is that the interior of the country to this day ſhows no ſigns of the reſults of thoſe efforts.

The tranſlation, and the notes that accompany it, make it unneceſſary for me to allude to the laborious reſearch and prolonged ſtudy which they have required. That labour has been willingly given, and will meet its reward if it contributes something to the materials for the Hiſtory of Africa which has yet to be written.

THOS. FOWELL BUXTON.

Warlies,
Waltham Abbey.

INTRODUCTION.

It was in the ſummer of 1878 that my attention was firſt directed to the work of Filippo Pigafetta. I was aſſiſting my huſband in the preparation of a ſhort work on Africa, which he has termed "The Loſt Continent and its Rediſcovery," and it became neceſſary to examine, as far as poſſible, into the records of the dealings with Africa of European nations. Mr. Major's work, "Prince Henry the Navigator;" Captain Burton's "Lands of Cazembe" and tranſlation of "Dr. Lacerda;" and Captain Elton's tranſlation of the "Chronicles of the Mozambique," have ſhown us the important part Portugal had played in tropical Africa. But our author, Pigafetta, we had not yet come in contact with.

Every ſtudent of African bibliography is, of courſe, acquainted with the work by name, but not many in theſe days have had the opportunity of ſtudying the work for themſelves. As may be ſeen, by reference to the Bibliographical Note, the work was, very ſoon after its publication, tranſlated into Engliſh by Abraham Hartwell, Rector of Toddington, Beds, and dedicated to Archbiſhop Whitgift. This quaint dedication I have placed at page xxiii. Hartwell's tranſlation forms the baſis of ſome portion of "Purchas, His Pilgrims," and "John Ogilvy's Account of Africa." A ſtill more intereſting uſe was made of it by Daniel De Foe. A writer in Macmillan's Magazine, in the year 1878, gives an account of the remarkable "Travels of Captain Singleton," and exprefles his furprife that the difcoveries of Stanley and others feem to have been anticipated fo far back as 1791. Apparently, unaware of the exiftence of our author's work, he fuppofes that Daniel De Foe had come in contact, perfonally, with Portuguefe travellers. To any one who has read both works it is manifieft that De Foe carries his hero, Captain Singleton, through the fcenes, and furrounds him with the events which Lopez defcribes in the pages of Pigafetta. The laft edition of the Encyc. Brit. ftates that, in a paper read before the Bombay Branch of the Afiatic Society, in 1863, Dr. Birdwood commented on the surprifing anticipation of recent difcoveries in Africa contained in the narrative of Captain Singleton. However, it is but fair to admit that the work of Pigafetta in the original Italian, and in the tranflation by Hartwell, is extremely fcarce; and we were indebted to the kindnefs of the Council of the Royal Geographical Society for permiffion to make free ufe of the Italian copy belonging to them. So much of intereft was revealed as the tranflation proceeded that, at Sir T. Fowell Buxton's requeft, it was refolved to tranflate the whole for private circulation. It was, however, thought that the book, with a certain amount of explanation and notes, would be interefting to a larger circle, and it is, therefore, given in its prefent form. Its preparation has involved an unexpected amount of labour in confulting and verifying authorities, and the tranflator afks the kind forbearance of the reader, for fhe feels that to do juftice to her tafk, required a fkilled and practifed hand. It was manifeft, on perufal of the work and ftudy of the large map prepared by Lopez, that fome confiderable portion of information had been obtained from other fources, which our knowledge of Portuguefe records was not fufficient to enable us to trace. Fortunately, however, at the very time that we were confidering this queftion, the materials needed were being prepared by a moſt competent authority, and the following extracts from M. Luciano Cordeiro's "L'Hydrographie Africaine" ſhow who the authors were whom Lopez muſt have ſtudied.

The Lyons Geographical Society had written for information to the Geographical Society of Liſbon. M. Cordeiro's reply takes the form of an eſſay; he ſays:—

"LISBON.

"SIR,

"THE Geographical Society of Liſbon has been agreeably ſurpriſed in hearing that the Geographical Society of Lyons is occupied in the ſtudy of a globe which, for many years, has remained forgotten in the principal library of your city.

"This globe, according to your courteous letter of the 23rd of February, 1878, and to which our Society directs me to reply, places the African Equatorial Lakes in an approximate poſition to that made known by the lateſt modern diſcoveries.

"Being aware that the Portugueſe, Duarte Lopez, had greatly contributed, by his voyages in Central Africa, towards furniſhing the Dominicans, who made the Lyons globe (to which you give the date 1701), with the information which enabled them to conſtruct it, you wiſh to have ſent you the works of Duarte Lopez, or, better ſtill, compiete accounts of the Portugueſe voyages, which, at the end of the 17th century, determined up to a certain point the theory which is in full vigour to-day, regarding the hydrographical ſyſtem of Africa and of the ſources of the Nile, a theory formerly forcibly combated on this laſt point by the French and other academies.

"Our Society will endeavour, with much pleaſure, to aid you in your intereſting reſearch, as well as to furniſh you with all the information, hiſtorical and geographical, which can be procured regarding the points to which you refer. Neverthelefs, I regret being unable to fend you the works, or, rather, the work of Duarte Lopez, or, more correctly, of Philip Pigafetta, in confequence of its being fo fcarce, that I hardly know of two copies in Portugal, and thofe incompletely printed, and belonging to the Government. . . .

"The full information you require, refpecting Portuguefe travels in Africa before the 18th century, would neceffarily involve too much labour. In order to fatiffy your immediate wants on the fubject, I fhall confine myfelf, therefore, to giving you haftily gathered details on the point occupying your attention at this moment. . . .

"Certainly, I can only attribute to entire ignorance of our language, and of our African geographical literature, the unjuft affertion of the eminent geographer, Monfieur Petermann, which fays, 'that the work of the Portuguefe in the exploration of Africa is almoft nil, and their information incomplete and inaccurate.' . . . You doubtlefs know, fir, that it was in Portugal, in the 14th century, the long and arduous campaign commenced for opening up Africa to fcience, civilization, and commerce, and that with an ardour which has, perhaps, never been furpaffed. If the Infante Dom Henrique inaugurated the difcoveries, King Dom João II. (1481—1495) was the real initiator of geographical exploration in the interior of Africa. It was, indeed, one of his chief defigns to make known the interior of the dark continent, to open a paffage acrofs Africa as far as the Indian Ocean, and to find, in fact, in thofe vaft regions what was then called the Empire of Prefter John. To this end, numerous expeditions were fent out, fo that the Portuguefe might difcover new parts of the coaft, and eftablifh themfelves there; and truftworthy men were to remain, by order of this illuftrious prince, amongft the natives, to cultivate friendly relations with them, and to puſh on into the interior under their guidance, ſo as to collect information of the people and country of thoſe parts. With this deſign, the king put in action the unceaſing deſire and zeal he had for the propagation of the Chriſtian religion, and gave preference to thoſe miſſionaries who had mathematical knowledge. But before that, our nation had already furniſhed modern African hiſtory with the firſt European explorer—*João Fernandes* (1445). Amongſt other expeditions, I will ſpecially refer in paſſing to thoſe of *Pero d'Evora* and of *Gonçallo Eannes* to *Tucoral* and *Tumbuctoo*, of *Mem Rodrigues* and *Pero d'Aſtuniga* to Timbuctoo and to Temala, King of the Foullahs; of *Rodrigo Rebello, Pero Reinel, João Collaco* firſt, and afterwards, in 1534, by command of the hiſtorian, *Barros*, of *Pero Fernandes*, to the interior of Senegambia, where the country is called *Mani-Manſa*—the *Mani-Mana* which Lopez places on the Upper Niger; of *Rodrigo Reinel, Diogo Borges*, and *Gonçalo d'Antas* to *Huadem*, in Adrar; of *Lucas*, an Abyſſinian, on the eaſt coaſt, in the country of Moſes, which was ſuppoſed to be the frontier of Abyſſinia, or Nubia; of *João Lourenço, Vicente Annes*, and *João Biſpo*, and of others to *Songo*, and to various parts of the interior of the country of the Mandingas and Foullahs. And at this point I may add, we poſſeſs very old and moſt intereſting works relating to expeditions acroſs Senegambia and in the interior of Africa. One of theſe, written by the clever explorer, *Captain Andre Alvares d'Almada*, dates from the ſecond half of the 16th century. . . .

"If to ſome extent the ſerious events of the reign of João II., and, later, the diſcovery of India, ſomewhat weakened intereſt in African diſcoveries, on the other hand, the growing ſettlement of the Portugueſe on that continent gave riſe, under commercial and religious influence, to wonderful explorations, which have continued, almoſt without interruption, to our own day. I may ſpecially refer to that of *Père Gonçalo da Silveira* to the interior of Monomotapa, in 1560; of *Franciſco Barreto* and *Vaſco Fernandes* to Chicova and Manica (1570—1573); of *Lopez* to the interior of Congo; and of *Rebello de Aragão* to the Kingdom of Angola, of which he was one of the firſt conquerors. In the 16th and 17th centuries, another important ſource of information on the interior of Africa is to be found in our extenſive navigation of the Atlantic and Indian Oceans, and from the large number of ſhipwrecks which occurred on the African coaſts. Frequently the ſhipwrecked ſailors remained for years amongſt the natives, accompanying them in their far-off expeditions. We find the King of Portugal already, in 1521, ſending an explorer—*Gregorio de Quadra*—to Congo, to go to Abyſſinia acroſs the continent; and in 1526, a Portugueſe, *Balthaſar de Caſtro*, who had lived for ſome time in Angola, ſending news to the King of Portugal from Congo, of an expedition being formed for the diſcovery of the principal ſource of that river, and begging to be entruſted with the conduct of it. In 1537, another Portugueſe, *Manuel Pacheco*, who evidently knew the country of Congo well, wrote on an identical project. . . . Two things ſhould be noticed—one is, that from 1516, the King of Congo became ſubject to Portugal; the other, that at the time of the Portugueſe ſettlement at Congo and Angola, the former kingdom extended much farther ſouth and eaſt than the actual territory bearing that name.

"Let us return to our ſubject, and ſee how Portugueſe geography of the 16th century underſtood and taught the chief elements of the hydrography of Africa, or what were the views on this ſubject which it enunciated.

"On a map, 'L'Inſularium illuſtratum Henriei Martelli

Germani,' which ſhows the Portugueſe diſcoveries on the weſtern coaſt of Africa up to 1489, the hydrography of the Nile retains the poſition Ptolemy gave it, but the *Rio Poderoſo*, which falls into the Atlantic with a large mouth, near the *pôta de padron*, recedes from, and approaches one of the central lakes of the Nile. Theſe lakes are fed by ſtreams of water from the Mountains of the Moon, ſituated in the middle of the continent.

"In the celebrated portulan of Juan de la Coſa (1500) we ſee a great lake, ſouth of the equator, giving riſe to the Nile, which flows direct north, having no communication with two leſſer lakes to the E. and N.E. of the other. *Duarte Pacheco Pereira*, who is ſuppoſed to have written in 1505, and who went to India, in 1503, with *Affonſo de Albuquerque*, ſays, in an intereſting nautical treatiſe, that the Zaire has its ſource in ſome mountains 50 leagues from the coaſt, but that it becomes very large from other rivers flowing into it. He ſays that the Nile riſes to the ſouth of the equator, that it forms two lakes near its ſource, and divides into two branches, which join again, forming the Iſland of Meroe. He ſays, alſo, of the Niger, that its courſe is long and its ſource unknown, but that it was believed to riſe from a lake of the Nile, near Tombouctoo.

"In the middle of the 16th century, when the colonization of Africa by the Portugueſe had greatly extended, the map of *Diogo Homem* (1558) has on it the Nile flowing by three principal branches from three lakes, two of which are in the middle of Ethiopia, between the Tropic of Capricorn and the equator, and almoſt in the ſame parallel of latitude; the third is under the equator to the N.E. of the others, and near the coaſt of Melinde, and on the frontier of the empire of Preſter John. . . .

"On one of the maps of the intereſting atlas arranged in

1563 by the Portugueſe, *Lazaro Luis*, one ſees a large lake as high up as the Kingdom of Quiloa, from which the Cuama, or Zambeſi, flows towards the S.E. by two arms; towards the S.E., the River Manhiſe; and towards the S., another river, without name, falls into Falſe Bay. . . .

"On the beautiful map of the world of Fernão Vaz Dourado, made at Goa in 1571, the ſame features are repreſented to a certain extent, with ſome modern modifications."

The next map to which M. Cordeiro draws attention is that of *Duarte Lopez*, which is deſcribed in the "Note." He paſſes now to the text of the geographers.

"One of the oldeſt and moſt intereſting ſources of information we poſſeſs relating to the Eaſt of Africa is, doubtleſs, that given by *Franciſco Alvares*, chaplain to the King of Portugal, and a native of Coimbra, who went to Abyſſinia, in 1520, with the embaſſy of *Dom Rodrigo de Lima*. . . . Already, before this, *Pero da Covilhan* had penetrated farther, and, according to Alvares, he had even been to the ſources of the Nile in the Kingdom of *Goyame*. Some who accompanied Alvarez—*Jorge d'Abren*, *Diogo Fernandes*, *Affonſo Mendes*, and *Alvarenga*—followed Preſter John in an expedition to the Kingdom of *Adea*, and almoſt got as far as Mogadoxo. . . .

"When, in 1552, Barros publiſhed his *Aſia*, our empire already extended along all the African coaſt, from Guinea to the entrance of the Red Sea, and the centres of Portugueſe colonization and exploration on the Ethiopian continent were already numerous and in a great ſtate of activity. Intercourſe with the interior was alſo carried on from the coaſt far inland, and the information thus directly, or indirectly gained, neceſſarily conſtituted an important baſis. In whatever elſe they might differ, theſe accounts ſeemed to agree perſiſtently on one point, and that was, the exiſtence of a great inland lake, or, rather, of a chain of great lakes, giving origin it might be to the Nile, or to the Zaire, or to the Zambesi. . . .

"On the south-east side, the idea of a great inland lake, with several rivers flowing out of it, and falling into the sea on that coast, dates from the first relations of the Portuguese with the natives of the Bay, which, after its exploration by Lourenço Marques, received the name of that navigator, instead of Bay of Lagoa, which the English have preserved under the odd name of Alagoa Bay. . . . We find stated in a work of the 16th century, the relation of the course of the Upper Nile to that of the Blue Nile, and, also, the origin of this last (Lake Tsana). This is the short history of *Miguel de Castanhoso*, who was with the famous expedition of *Dom Christovão da Gama* in Abyssinia. A contemporary of Castanhoso, *Dom João Bermudes*, and who was in those regions at the same period (1565), says, 'The Moorish king (of *Zeilah*) lives in a kingdom called *Dembia*, which the Nile crosses, and where it forms a lake 30 leagues long, and 5½ leagues broad. In this lake are several islands.' This is the Lake Tsana. Bermudes says of it, 'And this lake is not the one from which the Nile issues, as that river comes from much farther off; even more than 200 leagues above Damute.' It should be remarked that Bermudes lived in Damute, in his calling as a missionary. . . . In 1578, a Portuguese went to Africa, who, by his cultivated intellect, his boldness in refuting the geographical prejudices of his day, and the zeal he carried into his study of the interior of the great continent, was not so much an adventurer as a real explorer, animated with a desire to know and to unveil the mysterious heart of Africa. That Portuguese was Duarte Lopez.

"His revelations naturally caused less astonishment in Portugal than in the rest of Europe. Only a short time before the publication of "Pigafetta," *João dos Santos,* for example, had travelled over Eaſtern Africa, and actually corrected ſome of the matters contained therein. Yet the fact remains, that the obſervant talent of Lopez has given us one of the moſt remarkable maps of Africa. To all who have ſeen that map, the actual contour of African cartography, having regard to its central hydrography, is admirably laid down in its general features. . . .

"From what has been ſaid above, it would ſeem that the ſeveral notions of Portugueſe geography in the 16th century might be ſummed up as follows :—

"1. The lacuſtrian and general origin of the great African rivers—the Zaire, the Zambeſi, and the Nile; identity of origin by the ſimple ſuppoſition of the connexion of theſe rivers, or the lakes from which they flow, by a central ſtream flowing in the direction N.S., like the Lualaba in modern maps.

"2. Correction of Ptolomean geography; aſſertion of two great central lakes in a relative poſition N.S., beſides other lakes on N.E., near or under the equator; ſources of chief branches of the Nile, and others also on the N.S. and W., which explain the formation of the Niger, and of the Kaſſai, or Guango.

"3. Lengthened courſe of Zaire towards equator and ſouthwards, its firſt ſource in a ſouthern lake, or its identity with the central river S.N. (Lualaba).

"4. Approximate poſition of Nile baſin, extinction of the Nile of the Blacks, or of its connexion with Egyptian Nile. In looking at Lopez's map, one is inclined to ſay, 'This northern lake, under lat. 12° S., is the Bembe (Bangeweolo); this farther N. Tanganyika; Colve is the Ukerewe; Abiami the Abiad, or White Nile—as Barcena is Bahr Tſana; and Abagni, the Abavi, or Blue Nile; Tacuy, or the Nile, which flows from one to the other of the central lakes, is the

Luapala, or Lualaba, which Livingſtone alſo thought was the principal courſe of the great Egyptian river; the lake Chinonda, near Linzama, is the Tchad, &c.' Can all this deſtroy, in any degree, the glory of the great explorers? Not in the leaſt degree. . . ."

We believe that Mr. Major, one of the Hon. Secretaries of the Royal Geographical Society, was the firſt who drew attention to the work of Pigafetta, in a paper read by him, in June, 1867.

The above liſt of authorities, quoted by M. Cordeiro, is ſufficient to ſhow that Portugueſe travellers have penetrated the continent in almoſt every direction.

The map of Lopez ſhows, as a reſult of *their* obſervations, thoſe general features with which we have become familiar, as the reſult of *modern* travel.

The imperfect ſcientific knowledge of theſe earlier travellers, however, prevented their determining with accuracy the poſition of their various diſcoveries, and led them into errors with regard to the hydrography of the continent, which are apparent on their maps, and have led many to ſuppoſe that the information profeſſed to be given was largely drawn from their own imagination.

A general review of the travels and obſervations of the Portugueſe in Africa, ſupports thoſe who conſider that the work of modern travellers may be correctly termed the "Re-diſcovery of a Loſt Continent."

M. H.

ERRATA.

Page 15, line 10, *read* "south" *for* "south-west."
Page 20, line 15, *read* "shells" *for* "pigs."
Page 28, line 20, *omit* "even."
Page 29, line 1, *omit* "except."
Page 29, line 10, *for* "like the Africans" *read* "according to African custom."
Page 32, *read* "João" *for* "Joan."
Page 33, *read* "Dom João" *for* "Don Juan."
Page 33, line 16, *read* "de Novaes" *for* "di Novais."
Page 33, line 18, *read* "Dom" *for* "Don."
Page 41, line 23, *insert* "it" *before* "in."
Page 44, line 19, *omit* "they buy from."
Page 44, line 20, *insert* "buy" *after* "year."
Page 89, line 17, *read* "banishment of" *for* "dissensions among."
Page 98, line 14, *read* "Govea" *for* "Gova."
Page 114, line 24, *read* "horns" *for* "a horn."
Page 115, line 10, *read* "is" *for* "was."
Page 120, line 15, *read* "from India to Europe" *for* "to Europe from India."

To the most Gracious and Reverende Father in God, John by the providence of God, Lord Archbishop of Canterbury, Primate and Metropolitaine of all Englande, and one of the Lordes of her Majesties most honorable Privie Councell.

Most Reverend Father, my singular good and gracious Lorde: In all humble dutie I do offer to your grace this poor and slender present, in auspicium nascentis armi, *which I doe most hartely pray, may be as happie and prosperous both for your health and quiet governement as (thanks be to God) your latter yeares have beene. It is a description of a certain Region or Kingdome in* Africa, *called* Congo, *whose name is as yet scarce knowen to our quarters of* Europe, *neyther is there any great or solemne mention of it in any bookes that have beene published of that Third parte of the old* World. *And because this treatise doeth comprehend not onely the nature and disposition of the* Moci-Conghi, *which are the naturall inhabitantes and people of* Congo, *together with all the commodities and trafficke of that countrey, very fitte and pleasaunt to be reade, but also the religion which they professed, and by what meanes it pleased God to draw them from* Paganisme *to* Christianity, *I thought good thus to make it knowen to my countreymen of England, to the end it might be a president for such valiant English, as do earnestly thirst and desire to atchieve the conquest of rude and barbarous nations, that they doo not attempt those actions for commodity of Gold and Silver, and for other transitorie or worldly respectes, but that they woulde first seeke the Kingdome of God, and the salvation of many thousand soules, which the common enemie of mankinde still detayneth in ignorance: and then all other thinges shall be put in their mouthes aboundantly, as may bee seene by the* Portingalles *in this narration. Written it was by one* Philippo Pigafetta, *an Italian, and a very good Mathematician, from the mouth of one* Lopez *a* Portingal, *together with two maps, the one particular of Congo, the other generall of all* Africa, *and especially of the* Westerne *Coast, from* 34 *degrees beyond the* Æquinoctial *northwardes, downe along to the* Cape *of* Good Hope *in the* South, *and so upwardes againe on the* Easterne *Coast by the great Island of* Madagascar, *otherwise called the* Isle *of* S. Laurence, *til you come to the* Isle *of* Socotora, *and then to the* Redde Sea, *and from* Ægypt *into the inland* Southwards *to the Empire of* Presbiter-John. *I beseech your grace to accept of this my poore travell, and I will not cease to pray to Almightie God, according to my dutie, that hee will multiply many good years upon you, under the happy government of our most gracious and Soveraigne Lady Queene Elizabeth: whereunto the Church of* Englande *is bound to say, Amen. From your Graces house in Lambehith, the first of Januarie* 1597.

Your Graces most humble Servant at commaundement,

ABRAHAM HARTWELL.

TO THE

MOST ILLUSTRIOUS AND MOST REVEREND MONSIGNOR ANTONIO MIGLIORE,

BISHOP OF ST. MARK, AND COMMANDER OF THE ORDER OF THE HOLY GHOST.

IN the great day of puniſhments and rewards, our Saviour, of all the works which man in this world is expected to do, will not demand an account of any in compariſon with thoſe which relate to mercy, and the pious care and protection of the needy. And truly it ſeems innate in the human heart, and common even to uncivilized nations to have compaſſion on the afflicted and infirm, and to act towards them as benefactors. Moreover, the poor being found everywhere, ſo alſo hoſpitals and public refuges are raiſed for their benefit. Surpaſſing all others, however, in works of this kind is the City of Rome, where without doubt a greater number of charitable inſtitutions and refuges for the deſtitute have been raiſed than not only in any other city but in any other part of the world. Pre-eminent amongſt hoſpitals is that called the Hoſpital of the Holy Ghoſt, and of which Your Moſt Reverend Lordſhip was made Commander by the Holy Father Pope Sixtus V of happy memory, after your recall from the City of St. Mark, to which Biſhopric he had previouſly promoted you. That moſt wiſe prince ſaw ſuch an inſtitution needed the ſuperviſion of one who, in addition to high birth, was diſtinguiſhed for his prudence, moderation, and knowledge of the world; and who would alſo, in a ſpirit of ſtrict integrity, undertake to ſee finiſhed and reſtored all thoſe Houſes of Charity which from previous neglect had fallen into a ſtate of diſrepair, and place them thenceforth under rule and diſcipline. This work Your Moſt Reverend Lordſhip has excellently carried into effect. And truly it was providential that His Holineſs did impoſe on you this charge, not only on account of the above-mentioned matters, but alſo as for ſome years paſt, and particularly in the preſent one, the ſeaſons having been ſo bad, famine has prevailed to ſuch an extent that men fell by the wayſide, weak from lack of food. In ſuch overwhelming numbers have they crowded into this hoſpital, coming there from all parts, that never ſince its foundation, nor even during the time of peſtilence, was it remembered to be neceſſary before to cloſe the porches leading from the ſtreets, in order to make place for the beds of the ſick, which were not leſs than eight hundred in number. The number of infants increaſed in an incredible manner, so that even thoſe born in wedlock, in order that they ſhould not die of hunger, were by their own mothers, who were unable from weakneſs to give them natural nouriſhment, left secretly at the houſe of mercy. Some of theſe afterwards, when the ears of corn were ripe, and the time of the abundant harveſt had come, aſked for them back again. During which arduous ſtraits, when many died of contagious diſeaſes, none the leſs did you perſonally viſit that great multitude of ſick and ſuffering people, taking care that each day they ſhould be tended both in body and ſoul; being greatly upheld in this dangerous work by the praiſe beſtowed on your labours. Your forethought provided for the ſuſtenance at that time not only of the ordinary population, who, in conſequence of banditti infeſting the neighbourhood, lacked food, but alſo for the moſt miſerable and wretched in that crowd of ſuppliants. It was an act of charity alſo when, ſhortly before the above events happened, your Moſt Reverend Lordſhip preſented the Portugueſe Hermit, who had returned from Congo, to his Holineſs Pope Sixtus V of holy memory, commanding myſelf at the ſame time to arrange under certain heads the Hiſtory of the Kingdom of Congo, and of thoſe remote regions, where he had lived for twelve years, in order that they might be printed for public uſe. But for this gracious act we ſhould have been deprived of a very curious hiſtory, and one but little known to us. The Portugueſe related everything in his own tongue, from which, *viva voce*, it was tranſlated by myſelf into Italian; ſo that it is not matter of ſurpriſe if now and then the ſenſe of the words is altered from that uſed by authors in our language. His idiom not being well known, and his narrative much interrupted during its delivery, no doubt ſeveral words are uſed which do not belong to the court language. In ſhort, the account of ſubjects mentioned in theſe Books is ſingular, and ſuch as will prove uſeful to ſtateſmen, learned profeſſors, philoſophers, and geographers. The hermit promiſed fuller information on his return, to thoſe who might deſire it; and in the meantime we muſt be ſatisfied with this deſcriptive record, which I dedicate to your Reverence, who has ſpared neither fatigue nor aſſiduity in thus graciouſly procuring it for us. From Rome the 7th of August, 1591.

Your Moſt Reverend Lordſhip's Servant,

FILIPPO PIGAFETTA.

BOOK THE FIRST.

CHAPTER I.

VOYAGE FROM LISBON TO THE KINGDOM OF CONGO.

In the year 1578, when Don Sebaſtian, King of Portugal, ſet ſail for the conqueſt of the Kingdom of Morocco, Duarte Lopez, a native of Benevento, which is twenty-four miles diſtant from Liſbon, near the ſouth bank of the Tagus, alſo ſailed in the month of April for the Port of Loanda, in the Kingdom of Congo, going in a ſhip called S. Antonio, belonging to an uncle of his, which was laden with various merchandiſe for that kingdom. It was accompanied by a patacchio (which is a ſmall veſſel), to which he gave continual help, guiding it at night with lights, in order to prevent its miſſing the way his ſhip took. He arrived at the Iſland of Madeira, belonging to the King of Portugal, which is about 600 miles from Liſbon, and there remained 15 days in order to furniſh himſelf with proviſions and wine and alſo with various ſweetmeats, which are made there in great quantities and of excellent quality. There is an abundant ſupply of wine in this iſland, being perhaps the beſt in the world, which is ſhipped to various countries, but particularly to England. Leaving Madeira and paſſing by the Canaries, all belonging to Caſtile, he went into harbour in one of the Cape Verde Iſlands, called S. Antonio, which was not ſeen till they came upon it. From thence he ſailed to another, called S. Giacopo (St. Iago), which bears rule over the reſt, and is governed by the Biſhop and Governor, who reſide there; and here he took in proviſions. It is not our intention in this hiſtory to relate the number of the Canary Iſlands, which are many, nor to ſpeak of the Cape Verde Iſlands, nor to give their poſition, eſpecially as there is no lack of records affording a full account of thoſe regions. We aſpire to reach the Kingdom of Congo, and this ſhip was only here for a time on its paſſage. I ſhall merely add that theſe Cape Verde Iſlands were ſhown by Ptolemy to be the principal ones weſtward in the maps of his geography, together with the Cape called by him the Heſperium Cornu, and thoſe Macarie, or Bleſſed Iſlands, which we call the Fortunate Iſlands. The Portugueſe traded here with various merchandiſe, ſuch as coloured glaſs balls, and other little things much fancied by the people of thoſe parts, besides Holland cloths, caps, and knives, and in exchange, took back with them ſlaves, wax, honey, and various products, as well as linen cloths of many colours. Beyond theſe places, and right oppoſite them, on the mainland, are the countries and rivers of Guinea, and Cape Verde, alſo Sierra Leone, or Lion Mountain, ſo famous for its great ſize.

From the above-mentioned Iſland of St. Iago, they directed the ship's course towards Brazil ſo as to catch the wind, at the ſame time taking note of the weather prevailing in thoſe ſeaſons in order to accompliſh the voyage. There are two routes from the Iſland of St. Iago to Loanda, the port of the Kingdom of Congo; one being by the coaſt of Africa, the other by the high ſea. Sailing with the Tramontana wind, which blows in thoſe months, generally called North wind by the Portugueſe, Spaniards, French, and all the people of the North Sea, and directing the ſhip's courſe ſouth and ſouth-weſt, leaving behind the

Kingdom of Angola, to return there later, we attain the 27th or 29th degree beyond the equinoctial line in a direction oppoſite to that of our Pole, which in this hiſtory is ſtyled Antarctic, that is to ſay in oppoſition to the Arctic, which is our north, the Antarctic on the contrary being towards the ſouth. In this latitude of the oppoſite pole, navigators meet with winds known as Generali, or prevailing winds. Theſe, blowing during nearly the whole of our ſummer, and called by them North-eaſters, are with us in Italy between North-eaſt and Eaſt in the ſpring. They were known to the Venetians as Eaſters, and to the Greeks and Latins as Eteſii, or blowing at ſtated ſeaſons.

Sailing to within 29 degrees of the Antarctic, with the north wind, great advantage is gained; for, immediately the winds prevailing in those parts are felt, they turn the ſails, and ſteer the ſhip in a ſtraight courſe for Angola. Frequently, however, they loſe the track, having failed to catch theſe winds. It is beſt to go ſome time before and wait for this ſtrong wind, turning back afterwards, for in this way the longed-for haven will be gained. It is a remarkable fact that theſe winds blow ſteadily from the north to 29 degrees below the equinoctial line, and here ſtill more furious winds may drive one back, this occurring for ſix months of the year.

Now, on the above voyage, the ſhip St. Antonio, meeting theſe prevailing winds, ſteered north and north-weſt towards the Kingdom of Congo, and hauling the wind arrived after 12 days and nights at the Iſland of S. Elena (St. Helena), not looking for or even thinking of it. This iſland is ſo called from having been firſt diſcovered by the Portugueſe on the 3rd of May, the Feaſt of St. Helena. It is ſituated 16 degrees towards the Antarctic, is nine miles in circumference, being as ſmall as it is ſingular, and far from the mainland. From the ſea its mountains may be deſcried at thirty miles diſtance, and it is truly a miracle of nature, riſing out of that vaſt and tempeſtuous ocean, ſmall and alone, and affording ſafe anchorage to ſhips when they arrive diſabled and ſhort of water from India. It abounds alſo in proviſions.

The woods are thick with ebony-trees, which are uſed by the ſailors who come to the iſland. They alſo leave their names cut in the bark, the letters becoming larger with the growth of the trees. Very fine fruits grow without any cultivation, but the Portugueſe brought the vine there. Particularly in the vicinity of the little church, and of the ſailors' inns, there are groves of wild oranges, citrons, lemons, and large figs, and alſo of a peculiar kind of apple, which all the year round bears ripe and unripe fruit, like the orange-tree. It reſembles the pomegranate, with its large red ſeed and juicy pulp. This gift of being ripe all the year round Homer ſays is ſhared by divers fruits in the Iſland of Corfu. Wild goats, kids, and wild boars abound in the iſland, beſides other four-footed animals. There are alſo partridges, wild fowl, doves, and many kinds of large and ſmall birds. Both animals and birds are ſo tame as to have no fear of man. Thus they are conſtantly caught and killed, being afterwards ſalted with the ſalt formed by the waves of the ſea in natural caves in various parts of the iſland. In this way they are preſerved as food for the ſailors who land there.

The ſoil of this iſland is crumbled like red aſhes, but it is rich and fertile, and as ſoft under the feet as ſand, the trees ſhaking with the ſtrength of a man. But little labour is carried on, as after rain the fruits ſpring up from former ſeed. Radiſhes grow wild, and as large as a man's leg, being uſed as food. Cauliflowers, parſley, lettuce, pumpkins, peas, beans, and various kinds of pulſe abound in this fruitful ſpot, multiplying of themſelves, and needing no cultivation. Every ſhip brings fruits and herbs to the iſland, which, taking root, benignant nature gives the reward with uſury, preſerving them for the uſe of the ſailors. There are ſmall rivers of good water in this iſland, as well as ſafe anchorage for ſhips. Near the principal port ſtands a ſmall church, where the ornaments of the altar are taken care of; alſo the veſtments of the prieſts, and other things pertaining to the ſervice of Maſs. When ſhips paſs that way the prieſts go down to celebrate divine ſervice.

Here is alſo a retreat, where certain Portugueſe almoſt always live, two or three, or even one only remaining there; either on account of illneſs or miſdeeds. Some even voluntarily lead the life of a hermit in this ſolitary place, as penance for their ſins.

Excellent fiſh is found in abundance, the ſea ſeeming crowded with them, ſo that as ſoon as hooks are thrown into the water, great loads are brought out continuouſly.

Aſking why the Portugueſe had not taken care to fortify the iſland, it being ſo well placed for ſailors, and as if by the Providence of God planted there for the benefit of the Portugueſe navigators, which is fully told by Granata in the Symbol of Faith, written by him in Spaniſh and tranſlated by myſelf into Italian, I was told that it would ſerve no purpoſe to do ſo becauſe this iſland lies out of the way in going to India and is very difficult of acceſs, but in returning it lies in the way and is eaſily ſeen; ſo that it was not worth while to ſpend time and money and keep ſoldiers there to no profit, none but Portugueſe ſhips trading with it. To my reply, that the Engliſh for two centuries have, nevertheleſs, penetrated into theſe ſeas, one expedition being led by Drake, and the other during this year, 1588, by another pirate, alſo Engliſh, even more courageous than he, and named

Cavendiſh, who returned laden with riches; they ſaid that ſuch an undertaking could not be carried into effect in ſuch far-off ſeas, as everything of building material muſt be brought from Europe.

In fine, beſides all the above-mentioned advantages, the climate of this iſland is temperate, and the air pure and healthy; the winds are ſoft, and when men reach it ill and half-dead from the toils of the ſea, they ſpeedily recover and regain their former ſtrength.

From the Iſland of St. Helena they ſet ſail with the ſame weather, and arrived at the Port of Loanda, in the Province of Congo, in ſeventeen days, the wind having moderated a little. This port is a ſafe and very large one, being formed by an iſland of the ſame name, of which we ſhall ſpeak ſhortly. We have ſaid there are two paſſages from Cape Verde to Loanda. One has been now deſcribed, which, though not uſed afterwards, was for the firſt time navigated by that ſame ſhip which conveyed Duarte Lopez, and guided by Franceſco Martinez, the king's pilot, who knew theſe ſeas well and was the firſt to go by this way. The other is by the coaſt of the mainland. Sailing from the Iſland of St. Iago, and onwards to Cape delle Palme (C. Palmas), they reach the Iſland of St. Thomas, ſo called becauſe it was diſcovered on the feaſt of that apoſtle. It lies under the equinoctial line, and is 180 miles from the mainland, right oppoſite the River Gaban or Cloak (R. Gaboon), which has that ſhape, and whoſe port is forecloſed by an iſland lying at the mouth of the river. The Portugueſe come to this river in ſmall boats from the Iſland of St. Thomas, bringing ſuch commodities as they carry to the coaſt of Guinea, and taking in exchange ivory, wax, honey, palm oil, and negro ſlaves. Near the Iſland of St. Thomas, towards the north, lies another, called Il Prencipe (Prince's Iſland), 105 miles diſtant from the mainland, having the ſame products and trade as that of St. Thomas, but leſs in ſize. The Iſland of St. Thomas is ſomewhat round in form, being ſixty miles broad, and 180 in circumference. It is very rich, carries on a large trade, and was taken poſſeſſion of by the Portugueſe when they commenced the conqueſt of the Indies. It has many ports, but the principal one and where moſt ſhips enter is cloſe by the city.

The iſland produces a vaſt amount of ſugar and nearly every kind of food. In the city are ſeveral churches, and a biſhop reſides here, with numerous prieſts and a chaplain. A caſtle with a garriſon and artillery is near the port, to which it forms a battery, and this harbour can accommodate numerous ſhips. It ſeems ſtrange that when the Portugueſe firſt arrived here they found no ſugar planted, yet they brought it from other parts, together with ginger, which alſo took root and flouriſhed abundantly. The ſoil is moiſt and ſuitable to the growth of ſugar-cane, which flouriſhes and ripens with no other watering than the dew which falls in the morning like rain, and moiſtens the earth. There are in the iſland more than ſeventy buildings, or rather preſſes, for preparing ſugar; and every building has ſeveral houſes round it, ſo forming a village, with nearly 300 perſons given to this work. About forty large veſſels are laden with ſugar every year. It is true that ſince that time the worm like ſome plague—has deſtroyed the roots of the ſugar-cane, ſo that now from forty, five or ſix veſſels only are laden with ſugar, and thus it comes to paſs that it is ſo dear in thoſe countries.

The Iſland of St. Thomas trades with the people of the mainland, who frequent the mouths of the rivers. The firſt of theſe rivers is that called after Fernando di Poo, who firſt diſcovered it, and lies 5 degrees towards our pole. Over againſt its mouth riſes an iſland of the ſame name, 36 miles off. The ſecond river is Bora, or Dregs, the next, del Campo, the fourth, S. Benedetto, the fifth, the River Angra, at the mouth of which is an iſland called Coriſco, that is to ſay, thunder; and all theſe traffic in the ſame kind of merchandize as thoſe already mentioned.

But to return to the voyage from St. Thomas. Sailing ſouth from thence we find Cape lupo Gonzale (Cape Lopez), which is 1 degree beyond the equinoctial line, towards the Antarctic Pole, and 105 miles from the above-mentioned iſland. From thence ſhips ſail with winds off land, and conſtantly hugging the coaſt, and caſting anchor every day in a ſheltered place, or behind ſome point, or in ſome port, they at laſt reach the mouths of the greateſt river in Congo, called Zaire in that tongue, but which ſignifies I know, that is Sapio in Latin. From this point to the Port of Loanda is a diſtance of 180 miles. Theſe are the two paſſages by ſea from the Iſland of St. Iago (which is one of thoſe Cape Verde Iſlands already mentioned), the firſt having but a little while ago begun to be frequented.

CHAPTER II.

OF THE KINGDOM OF CONGO, AND ITS INHABITANTS.

It is now time to ſpeak of the Kingdom of Congo, and of all that relates to it. The centre of the Kingdom of Congo is ſituated 7 degrees and two-thirds from the equinoctial line, towards the Antarctic pole, at the point where the City of Congo lies; ſo that it is in the region conſidered uninhabitable by the ancients, and known as the Torrid Zone; that is, the girdle of the earth, burnt by the heat of the ſun.

This, however, is a miſtake, for the ſituation is good, the climate temperate beyond belief, and the winter much like the autumn ſeaſon in Rome. The inhabitants do not wear furs, nor change their apparel, neither have they fires, nor is it colder on the mountains than in the plains. The winter is generally warmer than ſummer, on account of continual rainfall; and eſpecially about two hours before and after midday the heat is almoſt inſupportable.

The men and women are black, ſome approaching olive colour, with black curly hair, and others with red. The men are of middle height, and, excepting the black ſkin, are like the Portugueſe. The pupils of the eyes are of various ſhades, ſome black, others of the colour of the ſea. Their lips are not large like the negroes, and their countenances vary, like thoſe of people in our countries, for ſome are ſtout, others thin, and they are quite unlike the negroes of Nubia and Guinea, who are hideous. The days and nights there are nearly equal, only varying a quarter of an hour all the year round. The winter in that country, ſpeaking generally, commences at the ſame time as our ſpring, that is to ſay, when the ſun enters the northern ſigns, in the month of March; and when our winter commences, and the ſun enters the ſouthern ſigns in the month of September, then their ſummer begins. During their winter the rain falls for five months almoſt continually, that is in April, May, June, July, and Auguſt, with few days of intermiſſion from tremendous ſhowers, for even the drops are ſo large as to be extraordinary; and by this means the earth is refreſhed after the dry ſeaſon, when no rain falls for ſix months. And when the earth is ſoaked with moiſture, then the rivers become filled again beyond all belief, and their ſtreams run through all the land.

The winds which blow in thoſe regions during the above-named months are the ſame which Cæſar calls by the Greek word Eteſii, that is, occurring annually. Theſe winds are marked in the compaſs as blowing from north to weſt and alſo ſouth-weſt. They drive the clouds to the tops of the high mountains, where, being hurled together with great force, they naturally are reſolved again into water, from which it is ſeen that clouds ſettle on the loftieſt heights at the time when it uſually rains. Hence occurs the overflow of thoſe rivers which riſe in Ethiopia, eſpecially that of the Nile and others, which run into the eaſtern and weſtern oceans. And in the Kingdoms of Congo and Guinea, through which the Niger flows (ſo called by the ancients, but known in modern times as the Senegal), this river overflows at the ſame time as the Nile, and pours its waters towards the weſt, to the right of the Cape Verde Iſlands. The Nile flows northward from the Iſland of Meroe, in Egypt, watering thoſe regions where barrenneſs and ſolitude prevail. Now as it only rains in Congo and Ethiopia at certain ſeaſons of the year, the overflow of the rivers is not extraordinary, being no new event. But in the far off and dry countries, like Egypt, where (excepting Alexandria and that region), it never rains, it is conſidered marvellous that ſuch an enormous quantity of turbid water ſhould come from diſtant regions, at a ſet time, and without fail; thus refreſhing the earth, and giving food to man and beaſt. On this account the ancients ſacrificed to the Nile, calling it, as is told in the 4th Book of Ptolemy, ἀγαθὸς δαιμόνιος, or the good god. Even to this day certain Chriſtians conſider it a miracle, ſince without theſe waters the people would periſh from hunger, as (ſays St. John Chryſoſtom) their lives depend on the riſing of the river.

So that theſe Eteſian winds, known to the Portugueſe as Generali, and which blow during our ſummer and in thoſe countries in winter, drive the clouds to thoſe very high mountains, where they are diſperſed again in rain. By reaſon of theſe rains, the winter there (as has been ſaid) is leſs cold, the water in thoſe hot regions generating warmth.

This is, then, the cauſe of the overflow of the Nile, and of other rivers under thoſe ſkies, concerning which the ancients, however, were in ſo great doubt, that they invented many fables about them. But in their ſummer, which is our winter, the winds blow diametrically oppoſite to thoſe above mentioned, that is, from ſouth-weſt to north-eaſt according to the compaſs. Without doubt, they muſt be extremely cold, coming from the oppoſite Antarctic pole, but on that very account they afford cooling breezes to thoſe regions, as do our own winds in ſummer in our country.

And although there theſe winds temper the heat of the atmoſphere, yet to us they bring torrents of rain. All this happens through a certain natural diſpoſition of the earth, which is regulated by the ſkies, and climate, under the Providence of God, who has ordered the heavens and the courſe of the ſun and of the other planets in ſuchwiſe, that every country in the world participates in their light, in equal proportion, both in cold and heat, all the year round. It is certain, alſo, that the heat would be inſupportable in the countries of Ethiopia and Congo, and thoſe adjacent to them, if theſe winds did not ſo refreſh and cool, that at night it is neceſſary to uſe two coverings. The ſame benefit is experienced from them by the people living in the iſland of Candia, and by thoſe in the Iſlands of the Archipelago, of Cyprus, of Aſia Minor, of Syria, and of Egypt, who are invigorated by theſe winds, ſo that they may well be called, as they are in Greek, *ζοήφορι*, that is, bringers of life.

It muſt alſo be remembered that in the mountains of

Ethiopia, of Congo, and of the ſurrounding regions, no ſnow ever falls, not even on the ſummits, excepting towards the Cape of Good Hope and on certain mountains ſpoken of by the Portugueſe, as Sierra Nevada, that is, ſnow mountains. Neither ſnow nor ice are found in the Kingdom of Congo, where they would be eſteemed more coſtly than gold, to mix with drinks of various kinds.

So that the rivers are not ſwollen by melting ſnows, but by the clouds pouring down rain during the five months of April, May, June, July, and Auguſt. Theſe rains commencing ſometimes fifteen days earlier, and at others fifteen days later, is the reaſon why the riſing of the Nile, ſo longed for by the people in Egypt, takes place late or early.

CHAPTER III.

CONCERNING THE COLOUR OF THE CHILDREN OF PORTUGUESE WHOSE MOTHERS ARE NATIVES OF CONGO.

It was thought by the ancients that the colour of the ſkin when black was cauſed by the heat of the ſun, as the nearer one approached the hot countries of the ſouth, mankind became darker, and on the contrary towards the north they became fairer, like the French, Germans, Engliſh, and others. Nevertheleſs, it is a fact that under the equinoctial line one finds people of light complexion as for inſtance in the kingdoms of Melinda and Mombaſa, and in the iſland of St. Thomas. The laſt has the ſame climate as thoſe places, and was firſt peopled by the Portugueſe, being formerly uninhabited. For more than 100 years their deſcendants have not only been fair, but have become more and more ſo.

So that as the children of the Portuguese, whose mothers were natives of Congo, have this complexion, Duarte Lopez gives it as his opinion that the black skin is not a result of the sun's influence, but has its origin in the blood, and, assuredly, his opinion is confirmed by Ptolemy, who, in his map of Libia, makes the Ethiopians white, and in his language they are called *Λευκαιθιοπες*, or White Ethiopians. Elsewhere he makes mention also of white elephants being found in those parts.

CHAPTER IV.

OF THE CIRCUMFERENCE OF THE KINGDOM OF CONGO, ITS DIVISIONS, AND BOUNDARIES.

THE Kingdom of Congo has four divisions. The western bathed by the ocean, the northern, eastern, and southern. Its boundary by the sea-coast commences at the Bay called seno delle Vacche, 13 degrees on the antarctic side, and following the coast-line towards the north side reaches to 4½ degrees, near the equinoctial line, a distance of 630 miles. This Bay is a moderate-sized port, but good, and capable of holding several vessels. It is so called because all round that region herds of kine are pastured; the land is flat and yields abundance of produce. Several kinds of precious metals, especially silver, are found and publicly sold, and the kingdom is subject to the King of Angola.

Farther on flows the river Bengleli, where a vassal of the King of Angola rules, and around the said river extends a region similar to the above-named country. A little farther is the River Songa, ſo called by the Portugueſe, becauſe for a diſtance of 25 miles the river preſents no variety. The River Coanza follows next, and iſſues from a ſmall lake, fed by a certain river flowing from the great and firſt lake, which gives origin to the Nile, of which in another part of this book we ſhall ſpeak. This river is two miles wide at its mouth, and navigable with ſmall boats againſt the current of the river for nearly 100 miles, but has no harbour.

It is worthy of remark that all this country which uſed to be ſubject to the King of Congo, is now under the abſolute rule of the governor of the province we have deſcribed, who profeſſes to be an ally and not a vaſſal of the king, but to whom he ſends preſents from time to time by way of tribute. The Port of Loanda, beyond the River Coanza, at an altitude of 10 degrees, is ſaid to be made by an iſland called Loanda, meaning, in the native tongue, flat country, and devoid of mountains, as it hardly riſes out of the water, and is formed from the ſand and mud which are depoſited by the ſea and the River Coanza, whoſe ſtreams meet here. It is about 20 miles long, and at the moſt a mile wide, in ſome parts the diſtance acroſs being only a bow-ſhot. A curious thing is that when digging in the ſand at the foot of two or three palm-trees, growing on it, the ſweeteſt water in the country is found. More than this, when the tide recedes this water becomes brackiſh, but on the tide flowing again it regains its ſweetneſs. The ſame thing happens in the iſland of Cadiz, in Spain, according to the teſtimony of Strabo.

This iſland furniſhes the money uſed by the King of Congo and the neighbouring people; for along its ſhores women dive under water, a depth of two yards and more, and, filling their baskets with ſand, they ſift out certain ſmall ſhell-fiſh, called Lumache, and then ſeparate the male from the female, the latter being moſt prized for its colour and brightneſs.

Theſe Lumache are found along all the coaſts of Congo, but thoſe of Loanda are fineſt, being tranſparent, and in colour ſomewhat like the chryſolite, with other kinds, not as greatly valued. It muſt be remembered that gold, ſilver, and other metals are not valued, nor uſed as money in theſe countries; and ſo it happens that with gold and ſilver in abundance, either in maſs or in coin, yet nothing can be bought except with Lumache. In this iſland are ſeven or eight towns, known in the language of the country as Libata. The principal one, called il Santo Spirito, is where the Governor reſides, who is ſent from Congo to adminiſter juſtice, and amaſſes riches from theſe Lumache. Here are alſo goats, ſheep, and wild boars, which though at firſt tame have become wild, and live in the woods. A large tree, called Enzanda, grows here; it is always green, and endowed with wonderful qualities, as from its branches, which ſpread upward, deſcend others, like threads, and theſe, forcing themſelves into the earth and taking root, other trees multiply in like manner. Inſide the outermoſt bark of this tree a ſubſtance is found, which, when cleanſed and prepared for uſe, makes clothes for the pooreſt of the people. In this iſland the boats are made from the trunks of palm-trees joined together. They have prow and ſtern, oars and ſails, and are uſed by the natives for catching fiſh, which abound along theſe coaſts; they alſo ſail in them to the mainland. In that part of the iſland looking towards the mainland trees grow in certain ſhallows near the ſhore, which are ſeen when the tide ebbs; and oyſters cling to their roots, containing very good food. They are as large as a man's hand, and well known to the people of the country, who call them Ambiziamatare, that is, rock-fiſh.

From the ſhells of the oyſters, when burnt, good lime is made for building material; and from the bark of the tree called Manghi, which reſembles cork, ſkins of oxen are tanned and made into ſoles for ſhoes. In ſhort the iſland produces no corn, or vines, but proviſions are brought from the parts round about and given in exchange for theſe Lumache; for although in other parts barter is with metals, here it is with Lumache. So that from this one can underſtand how not only in the Kingdom of Congo, but in Ethiopia, Africa, and China, and in ſome parts of India, money is uſed of a different kind from gold, ſilver, or copper, or a mixture of theſe. For in Ethiopia pepper is the currency, in Timbuctoo, which is near the River Niger called Senegal, they uſe cockle-ſhells, amongſt the Azanaghi Porcelette are money, and in the Kingdom of Bengal pigs and metals together form the currency. In China, certain ſhell-fiſh, alſo called Porcelette, and in other places paper ſtamped with the king's ſeal; and bark from the mulberry-tree take the form of money. So that metal is not the ſtandard for obtaining the value of merchandiſe in every part of the world, as it is in Europe, and in ſome other parts.

This iſland, in its narroweſt part, is near the mainland, and the people ſometimes ſwim acroſs its channel. Several ſmall iſlands ſituated in this ſtrait are uncovered at low water and again covered by the tide. Large trees grow in them, and it is ſaid oyſters are found on their roots.

Near this iſland, and towards the coaſt, numerous black whales are ſeen ſwimming. Theſe fight with each other, and when dead are thrown by the waves on the beach, like a ſtranded veſſel. The natives then go with their boats to fetch and to take the oil from them, which they mix with pitch and uſe for their veſſels. On the backs of theſe creatures grow quantities of ſhell-fish, like ſnails and whelks, and Don

Lopez affirms having ſeen this himſelf, adding that he does not believe they produce amber, for along all the coaſt of Congo, where ſo many of them exiſt, neither ambergriz nor any other amber is found, and if furniſhed by theſe creatures ſome muſt, of neceſſity, be found on theſe ſhores.

The entrance of the principal port is towards the north, being on that ſide half a mile large, and of great depth. On the mainland, to the right, is the city of S. Paulo (St. Paul de Loanda), entirely inhabited by Portugueſe, with their wives, whom they brought from Spain. It has, however, no fortreſs.

All this channel is very full of fiſh, eſpecially of ſardines and anchovies; and in winter the number is ſo great that they even leap on land. There are alſo ſoles, ſturgeon, barbel, and every kind of excellent fiſh, including large crabs in great abundance, and ſo wholeſome that the greater part of the people on theſe ſhores make them their chief food.

The River Bengo, which is large and navigable for 25 miles, runs into this channel, and, together with the River Coanza, of which we ſpoke before, forms the Iſland of Loanda, their waters meeting and depoſiting ſand, and ſo this iſland is raised. Farther on flows another and larger river, called Dande, which can float veſſels of 100 tons; and beyond it the River Lemba, which has no harbour, and into which no ſhips enter. Very near to this is the River Ozoni, which flows from the ſame lake as the Nile, and has a port. Next comes the River called Loze, without a port; and another great one with a harbour, called Ambriz, flowing four leagues from the royal city of Congo. Laſt of all is the River Lelunda, ſignifying trout fiſh. It bathes the foot of the mountain on which ſtands the royal city of Congo, called Oteiro by the Portugueſe. This River Lelunda, iſſuing from the ſame ſmall lake as the Coanza, and another river running into it, which comes from the great lake, can be croſſed on foot in the dry ſeaſon. The great River Zaire (R. Congo) comes next, being the largeſt in the Kingdom of Congo. It takes its riſe from three lakes, one ſource coming from the large lake out of which the Nile iſſues, the ſecond from the ſmall lake above mentioned, and the third from the ſecond great lake formed by the Nile. Aſſuredly it needs no ſmaller ſtreams to increaſe its ſize, being at its mouth 28 miles wide. When at its full height, it ſends freſh water into the ſea a diſtance of 40 or 50, and at times even 80 miles, which ſerves as refreſhment to travellers, who know the place from the turbid waters. It is navigable for 25 miles, with large boats, till it reaches a ſtrait between rocks, where the waters pour down with ſuch tremendous noiſe as to be heard nearly eight miles off. This place is called by the Portugueſe Cachivera, that is, a fall or cataract, as it reſembles that of the Nile. Between the mouth of the river and the fall are many large iſlands, covered with well-inhabited towns, the rulers of which are ſubject to the King of Congo. Theſe lords, when at enmity with one another, fight amongſt themſelves from time to time. They uſe their boats to fight from, which are hollowed out of the trunk of a very large tree, called Lungo. Their largeſt veſſels are cut out of the wood of a tree called Licondo, which is ſo enormous that ſix men cannot compaſs it with their arms, being long in proportion, ſo that one of them will carry about 200 persons. They row theſe boats with their oars, which are not tied to loops, but are held in the hand, and with them they ſtrike the water quickly. Every one has his oar and his bow, and whilſt fighting they lay down the oar and take the bow, but have no other way of turning and managing their boats than by uſing theſe oars. The firſt of theſe iſlands, and a ſmall one, is l'Isola de

Cavalli, becaufe here are found feveral of thofe animals called by the Greeks Hippopotami, that is, river-horfes. The Portuguefe live in a fmall town in this ifland, by way of fecurity, and their boats pafs to the mainland, on the fouth fide of the river, to a place called the port of Pinda, and where all veffels coming there anchor.

In this river are various kinds of creatures, and amongft them large crocodiles, called by the natives Caiman, also the river-horfe above mentioned, and a fimilar one, having as it were two hands, with a tail like a target. It is called Ambize Angulo, that is, fifh pig, for it is fat like the pig, and the flefh is very good, lard being made from it; nor does it tafte of fifh, although it is one. This pig never leaves frefh water, but eats grafs on the banks, having a mouth like the muzzle of an ox. Some of thefe fifh weigh as much as 500 pounds. The fifhermen chafe them in their boats, obferving where they feed, then ftick them with hooks and forks, and, when dead, draw them out of the water. When cut in pieces they carry them to the king, upon pain of life to whoever omits to do so. The fame occurs when trout and tench are caught, and alfo another kind of fifh, called Cagongo, which refembles falmon, although its colour is not red. This fifh is fo fat as to put out the fire whilft being cooked. Other fifh found here, and called royal fifh, is all carried to the king; any one omitting to do fo being under penalty of very fevere punifhment. To thefe fifh many more might be added which it is not neceffary to name. Beyond the River Congo is another, called by the Portuguefe la Baia de las Almadias, that is, Gulf of Boats, becaufe great numbers of boats are built there, the thick forefts furnifhing excellent timber, of which the neighbouring people make ufe for that purpofe. At the mouth of this bay are three iflands; a large one in the middle of the channel, which ſerves as a port for ſmall veſſels, and two leſſer, none of which are inhabited. Still farther on we find a ſmall river, called de las Boreras Roſſas, as it paſſes between mountain rocks whoſe ſoil is vermilion colour. Here riſes a very high mountain, which extends inland, and is called by the Portugueſe la Sierra Complida, that is Long Mountain. Continuing onwards we find two bays of the ſea in the ſhape of a pair of ſpectacles, where is a good harbour, and this is called Baia d'Alvaro Gonzales, that is Bay of Alvaro Gonzales. From this point are mountains and ſhores not worthy of mention, which extend as far as the cape called Caterina by the Portugueſe (Cape S. Catherine), which is the boundary of the Kingdom of Congo, towards the equinoctial line, and diſtant from the latter two and a half degrees, equal to 150 Italian miles.

CHAPTER V.

OF THE NORTHERN SIDE OF THE KINGDOM OF CONGO AND ITS BOUNDARIES.

Now, another boundary of the Kingdom of Congo begins at Cape Caterina on the north ſide, and terminates on the eaſt at the junction of the Rivers Vumba and Zaire, a diſtance of more than 600 miles. Beyond this boundary northwards, and under the equinoctial line, along the ſea-ſhore, and for about 200 miles inland, including the afore-mentioned Gulf of Lope Gonzales, the people called Bramas inhabit a territory now known as the Kingdom of Loango, and their king is called Maniloango, that is, King of Loango. The country abounds in elephants, and their teeth are exchanged for iron, of which the people make arrowheads, cutlaſſes, and ſimilar weapons. Here alſo they weave cloth from the leaves of the palm-tree, to which we ſhall refer later in this hiſtory. The King of Loango is at amity with the King of Congo, but it is ſaid was formerly his vaſſal. The people uſe the rite of circumciſion like the Hebrews, as is the cuſtom of all heathen in thoſe countries. They are friendly amongſt themſelves, but fight with the neighbouring tribes at times, reſembling the people of Congo in every particular. Their weapons are long ſhields, which almoſt entirely cover the body, and are made from the tough ſkins of a certain animal called Empachas, which is ſmaller than the ox, with horns like a goat, and is ſtill found in Germany, where it is called Dant. From theſe parts and from Congo the ſkins are taken to Portugal, and from thence to Flanders, where they are dreſſed and made into jerkins, corſelets, and cuiraſſes, to which they give the name of Dant. As weapons of offence this people uſe long iron ſpears, reſembling a partiſan or the old Roman pilum. This ſpear is of a convenient length for throwing, and, to ſecure greater force, a wooden knob is placed in the middle of the weapon to hold it by. They alſo carry daggers or poniards made like an iron dart.

Beyond the Kingdom of Loango the people called Anziques live, of whom truly ſtrange ſtories are told, and well-nigh incredible from their horrible character, for they eat human fleſh, and even their own relations if neceſſity occurs.

This country is bounded on the weſt coaſt by the region inhabited by the people of Ambus, on the north by the Nubian Deſert, and certain African tribes, and on the eaſt by the ſecond great lake from which the River Congo takes its riſe in the Anzicana region, and is divided by that

River from the Kingdom of Congo. In the River Zaire are many iſlands (as has been ſaid) ſcattered from the lake downwards, ſome of which are under the rule of the Anziquez, who trade by means of this river with the people of Congo.

In this Kingdom of the Anziques are ſeveral copper-mines, and a great quantity both of red and grey ſandal-wood. The red is called Tavilla, and the grey, which is moſt valuable, Chicongo. A powder is made from it, which emits a delicious perfume. Medicines alſo are prepared from it, the natives mixing the powder with palm oil, and anointing the entire body to preſerve themſelves in health. They put it on the pulſe, and uſe it as a remedy for the French malady, called in that tongue Chitangas. The Portugueſe, however, diſſolve it in vinegar for their own uſe. Some aſſert that this grey ſandal-wood is the very Lignum Aquila, which grows in India, and Duarte Lopez affirms that the Portugueſe proved it to be ſo by putting it on burning coals, and inhaling the fumes when ſuffering pain in the head. The virtue is only in the pith and innermoſt part of this tree, the reſt being of no value.

The Anzichi make linen cloths from the palm-tree in various forms and colours; and alſo ſilk ſtuffs, of which we ſhall ſpeak later. They are ſubject to a king who has ſeveral princes under him, and are a very active, warlike, and bold people in battle, fighting on foot. Their weapons differ from thoſe of all the ſurrounding people, and are ſhort wooden bows, covered with ſerpents' ſkins of divers colours, being of ſuch wonderful workmanſhip as to ſeem made of one piece, and this is done to ſtrengthen the bow and give firmer hold. The ſtrings are made of ſmall wooden twigs, like canes, but as firm and pliable as thoſe which the cavaliers of Portugal uſe for beating their palfreys. Theſe canes, which are red, and alſo ſomewhat black, grow in the country of the Anzichi and alſo in Bengal, through which kingdom the River Ganges flows. Their arrows are ſhort and ſlender, made of hard wood, and are carried in the bow hand. Theſe people ſhoot with ſuch dexterity that 28 arrows, and more, are diſcharged before the firſt falls to the ground; and it is ſaid, at times, their ſkilful archers can kill a bird flying. Beſides theſe weapons they uſe alſo a ſort of poleaxe of curious ſhape, the handle being half the length of the blade. At the lower end is a knob by which to hold it ſecurely in the hand, alſo covered with the ſnake-ſkin above mentioned. The head ſhines brightly, being faſtened with copper pins in the wood, and at one end it has a ſharp edge like a hatchet, in the form of a half-circle, and at the other a hammer. In fighting, they defend themſelves from their enemies' arrows with this weapon inſtead of a ſhield, and turn it every way with ſuch readineſs that they ward off the ſhafts aimed at them. They wear alſo ſhort daggers, in ſcabbards covered with ſerpents' ſkins, and made like knives with a haft, which they carry flung acroſs them. Their belts are of various kinds, but warriors uſe thoſe made of elephants' hides, three fingers broad, and two thick. They are difficult to make, having to be put through great heat to make them round, and are faſtened with buckles croſs-ways. Theſe people are wonderfully active and nimble, leaping up and down the mountains like goats, very hardy, without fear of death, ſimple, ſincere, and loyal, and, indeed, the Portugueſe have greater confidence in them than in any other tribes. So that Duarte Lopez well says, If theſe Anziquez became Chriſtians (being thus faithful, truthful, loyal, and ſimple, giving themſelves even to death for the glory of the world and their fleſh to their princes for food, if it would pleaſe them), how much more from their hearts would they ſuffer martyrdom for the name of our Redeemer,

Jeſus Chriſt, and nobly defend our faith and religion, both by teſtimony and example, in preſence of the heathen.

Duarte Lopez alſo tells us that in conſequence of this people being ſo cruel, they were not traded with, excepting in ſo far as they came to Congo, bringing ſlaves of their own tribes and from Nubia, a boundary of their country, with ſuch things beſides, for barter, as linen cloths, and elephants' teeth. They carry back with them ſalt, and the Lumache, uſed as money, alſo a larger kind of Lumache, found in the Iſland of St. Thomas, of which they make themſelves ornaments and charms, as well as goods brought from Portugal, including ſilk, linen cloths, glaſs, and ſuchlike. They uſe the rite of circumciſion, and one of their cuſtoms is, for every child, both male and female, to be marked on the face with various devices cut with a knife, nobles and common people bearing the ſame marks; of which we ſhall ſpeak in due order.

They have ſhambles for human fleſh, as we have of animals, even eating the enemies they have killed in battle, and ſelling their ſlaves if they can get a good price for them; if not, they give them to the butcher, who cuts them in pieces, and then ſells them to be roaſted or boiled. It is a remarkable fact in the hiſtory of this people, that any who are tired of life, or wiſh to prove themſelves brave and courageous, eſteem it great honour to expoſe themſelves to death by an act which ſhall ſhow their contempt for life. Thus they offer themſelves for ſlaughter, and as the faithful vaſſals of princes, wiſhing to do them ſervice, not only give themſelves to be eaten, but their ſlaves alſo, when fattened, are killed and eaten. It is true many nations eat human fleſh, as in the Eaſt Indies, Brazil, and elſewhere, but to devour the fleſh of their own enemies, friends, ſubjects, and even relations, is a thing without example, except amongſt the Anzichi tribes.

The uſual dreſs of theſe people is as follows: Men of the lower claſs are naked above the waiſt, wearing nothing on the head, but their locks are long and wavy. The nobles wear ſilk and other garments, and on the head ſmall red, and black caps, alſo velvet caps from Portugal, as well as others uſed in the country, and all are envious of being well dreſſed as far as they are able. The women are entirely covered from head to foot like the Africans, the poorer ſort having garments from the waiſt downwards. The noble ladies, and thoſe who are able, wear certain mantles, which are wrapped round the head, leaving the face free. Theſe alſo wear ſhoes and walk very nimbly, and are of fine ſtature, and pleaſant countenance. The poor go bare-footed. Their language is quite different from that of Congo, and the Anziquez always eaſily learn the Congo tongue, becauſe it is plain and clear, but the Congo people find it very difficult to learn that of the Anziquez. Having aſked what is the religion of this people, I was told they are pagans, but could find out nothing more about them.

CHAPTER VI.

OF THE EASTERN BOUNDARIES OF THE KINGDOM OF CONGO.

The eaſt ſide of the Kingdom of Congo begins, as has been ſaid, at the junction of the Rivers Vumba and Zaire, and a line drawn towards the ſouth, equally diſtant from the River Nile, which is on its left, takes in the high and uninhabited ſummits of the mountain called Cryſtal, great quantities of cryſtals of all kinds being found there. Paſſing on ſtill farther, it includes the heights called the Sun Mountains;

for although ſo high, they are never covered with ſnow, and are utterly deſtitute of vegetation. On the left riſe the Saltpetre Mountains, ſo called from that mineral being found there; and after croſſing the River Berbela, which iſſues out of the firſt lake, there terminate the ancient limits of the Kingdom of Congo on the eaſt. Thus the eaſtern boundary of this kingdom extends from the junction of the above-named River Vumba with the Zaire to Lake Achelunda and the country of Malemba, a diſtance of 600 miles. From this line which is drawn along the eaſtern boundary of Congo to the River Nile, and to the two lakes, of which we ſhall make mention preſently, a well-populated country extends for 150 miles, with mountains abounding in various metals, and where different kinds of cloth are made from the palm-tree. At this point of our hiſtory it is neceſſary to relate the wonderful manner in which the people of this and the adjacent countries make various kinds of ſtuffs, ſuch as velvets with and without nap, brocades, ſatins, taffetas, damaſks, and ſuchlike. None are made of ſilk as they have no knowledge of the ſilk-worm, and when ſilk robes are worn they are brought from our parts. But they weave their cloths from the leaves of the palm-tree, keeping the latter growing near the ground, and cutting and watering them yearly, ſo that every ſeaſon they may become more tender.

From theſe leaves, when prepared after their own manner, very fine threads are drawn, and delicate to a degree in ſtructure. The longeſt are moſt valuable, as from them are woven the largeſt pieces of cloth, on which various patterns are worked, the material having the appearance of velvet on both ſides. Damaſks alſo are made from them, worked in various patterns, as well as brocades, which are called high and low, and reckoned much more valuable than our brocades. The king only, and thoſe he pleaſeth, are permitted to wear this cloth. The largeſt pieces are uſed for brocades, as they are four or five ſpans long and three or four broad. They are called Incorimbas, which is the name of the country where they grow, and lies near the River Vumba. The velvets of the ſame width and length as the above are called Enzachas, the damaſks, Inſulas, the ſatins, Maricas, the taffetas, Tangas, and others, Engombos.

The largeſt pieces are made from lighter ſtuffs by the Anzichi, ſome being as much as ſix ſpans long, and five wide. Every one who poſſibly can dreſſes in theſe garments, for they have the quality of reſiſting water, and are very light. The Portugueſe alſo uſe them for tent cloths, as they are wonderfully proof againſt both rain and wind.

The above-mentioned boundary ſhuts in the Kingdom of Congo lying weſt of it, from which coaſt, with a line of equal diſtance farther eaſt, the Nile flows for about 150 miles, encloſing a country abounding in the afore-mentioned products, the territory of numerous lords, ſome of whom are ſubject to Preſter John, and others to the great King Moenemugi. Of this country we have nothing more to relate, excepting that it is said the people on the weſt of the Nile trade with the Kingdom of Congo, and along its ſea coaſts; and thoſe on its eaſtern ſide go through the Kingdoms of Moenemugi as far as the Gulfs of Mombaſa and Mozambique.

CHAPTER VII.

OF THE BOUNDARIES OF THE KINGDOM OF CONGO TOWARDS THE SOUTH.

THIS eaſtern coaſt terminates, as has been ſaid, at the great mountain, called dell' Argento, and there begins the fourth and laſt border of the Kingdom of Congo towards the ſouth, reaching from the aforeſaid mountain to il Golfo delle Vacche on the weſt, a diſtance of 450 miles.

This line paſſes through the middle of the Kingdom of Angola, having the Silver Mountains on its left. Beyond them, towards the ſouth, is the great Kingdom of Matama, independent and powerful, at times friendly and at other times at enmity with Angola.

The King of Matama is a pagan, and his kingdom extends from the above-mentioned boundaries to the River Bavagal on the ſouth, and very near the baſe of what are commonly called the Mountains of the Moon. On the eaſt it is bounded by the weſtern ſide of the River Bagamidri, and croſſes over the River Coari. The country abounds in mines of cryſtal and various minerals, and in every kind of food, for the climate is good. Notwithſtanding the people traffic with the neighbouring tribes, none the leſs do the Kings of Matama and Angola very often go to war with each other, as we have before mentioned.

This River Bagamidri divides the Kingdom of Matapa from that of Monomata, which lies towards the eaſt, and of which Joan de Barros has fully written in the firſt chapter of his tenth book.

Towards the ſea-coaſt are many lords who, although of inferior rank, uſurp the title of king. Not many harbours of importance are found along theſe ſhores. As we have frequently ſpoken of the Kingdom of Angola, it is now time to treat of it more fully, for, as has been ſaid, though formerly ruled by a governor under the King of Congo, this goyernor has, ſince the king became a Chriſtian, made himſelf abſolute ruler. Having uſurped all thoſe countries over which he bare rule, and in proceſs of time conquered ſome of the ſurrounding provinces, he is now a great and rich prince, and hardly leſs powerful than the King of Congo, to whom he pays tribute or not, according as he chooſes.

It came to paſs that after Don Juan II., of Portugal, planted the faith of Chriſt in the Kingdom of Congo, and the king became a Chriſtian, the Lord of Angola was always friendly towards him, being to ſome extent a vaſſal, and their people trading together. He ſent tribute every year to the King of Congo, and trade was carried on at the Port of Loanda between the Portugueſe and the people of Angola by permiſſion of the King of Congo. Slaves were bought and exchanged for other merchandiſe, all being ſent to the Iſland of St. Thomas, the trade here being united with that of St. Thomas, ſhips firſt calling at that iſland, and then going on to Loanda. Trade becoming ſucceſſful, they began to ſend veſſels themſelves from Liſbon to Angola, and alſo a governor, Paulo Diaz di Novais by name, to whom belonged this privilege on account of his anceſtors having firſt diſcovered this trade. To this Paulo Diaz, Don Sebastian, King of Portugal, conceded the power of conquering 33 leagues of country, beginning at the River Coanza, and going ſouthward inland, where he was to take all he could gain for himſelf and his heirs. Many other ſhips went with him, thus opening a great trade with Angola, which, however, was always directed to the Port of Loanda, where the above-mentioned veſſels unloaded. By degrees he penetrated to the mainland, forming a ſtation at a village called Anzelle, a mile from the River Coanza, ſo as to be more convenient and near to the Angola traffic. The trade having increaſed ſo far, and the Portugueſe and Congo people freely bringing their goods to ſell and barter at Cabazo, a place where the Lord of Angola lived, and about 150 miles from the ſea, the ſaid lord ordered that all the merchants ſhould be killed, and their goods forfeited, affirming that they had come there as ſpies, and to ſeize on the place. It was thought, however, he did it to gain poſſeſſion of their goods, for theſe people were not dreſſed as warriors but as merchants. And this happened in the ſame year that King Don Sebaſtian was defeated in Barbary. On account of this Paulo Diaz took up arms againſt the King of Angola, and, with the people he could aſſemble from amongſt the Portugueſe whom he found in thoſe parts, and two galleys, and other ſhips which he had in the River Coanza, he went ſtill farther on both ſides of the river, conquering and ſubjugating numerous lords by force of arms, making them friendly and ſubſervient. But the King of Angola ſeeing his vaſſals ſubmitting themſelves to Paulo Diaz, and the latter gaining territory, he gathered a great army to deſtroy him. Therefore Paulo Diaz appealed to the King of Congo for help, which he gave, by ſending him an army of 60,000 men, commanded by his couſin, Don Sebaſtian Manibamba, and alſo a captain, with 120 Portugueſe ſoldiers, who were in the country, and whom he paid for this enterpriſe. This army arranged to join that of Paulo Diaz, in order that they might together encounter the King of Angola, but arriving at the ſhore where they were to croſs the River Bengo, 12 miles from Loanda, and where they expected to find boats to carry the ſoldiers over, they found theſe boats were delayed, and as much time would have been loſt in conveying ſo many people acroſs, the army took the road on the oppoſite ſide of the river, where ſome diſtance in front they met the Angola people, poſted there to prevent their entrance into the country. The order of battle of the Mociconghi (for ſo the natives of Congo are called, as thoſe of Spain are called Spaniards) and of the Angola people is almoſt the ſame; for they both fight on foot, dividing their army into ſeveral companies, accommodating themſelves to the battle-field, wherever it may be, and carrying their banners and colours in the way we have already ſpoken of.

The movement of their troops in battle is regulated by various ſounds and rattling of arms, directed by the captain-general, and which, when heard in the midſt of the battle, ſignify if the troops are to attack, or to retire, to move forward, or wheel to left or right, or any other military movement. By theſe ſounds the orders of the general are diſtinctly underſtood, in the ſame manner as the drum and trumpet are with us. They uſe three principal ſounds in war. One proceeds from large kettle-drums, whoſe caſes are made from a ſingle piece of wood, and covered with leather, which they ſtrike with ſmall clubs of ivory. Another ſound is made by an inſtrument in the ſhape of a pyramid, but turned upſide down, as they are pointed at the bottom and wide at the top. This inſtrument has thin plates of iron, hollow inſide, and is like a bell turned upſide down. They are ſtruck with rods of wood, this being done inceſſantly to produce as hoarſe and warlike a noiſe as poſſible; even, at times, cracking them, to increase the horrible ſounds. The third inſtrument is made from elephants' tuſks, both large and ſmall ones, which being hollow they blow through a hole at the ſide like a flute, and not from the top, and they are arranged ſo as to ſound like a cornet, producing military and agreeable muſic, and ſuch as inſpires the ſoldiers with courage. Theſe three warlike inſtruments are large and ſmall, the large ones being carried with the captain-general, ſo that he may give the ſignal to the whole camp, the different corps and each captain of a troop having ſmaller ones, and ſounding the drums with their hands. So that on hearing the kettle-drums, or the cornet, or the third inſtrument, every part of the army reſponds with its own inſtruments, to ſhow the ſigns were underſtood, the under officers doing the ſame. And not only were theſe ſounds uſed as a general thing, but alſo in the act of fighting; for, during the ſkirmiſhes, brave men went with theſe inſtruments in front of the ſoldiers, dancing and beating the drums to encourage them, at the ſame time giving warning of any danger which threatened by the various ſounds.

The military dreſs of the Mociconghi lords is as follows: On the head a cap ornamented with cock's, oſtrich's, peacock's, and other feathers is worn, which makes the men ſeem taller and very formidable. Above the waiſt they are entirely naked, and hanging from both ſides of the neck are chains of iron with rings the ſize of a man's little finger, which they wear as if for military pomp. Below the waiſt they wear breeches of cloth, or thin ſtuff, and over that a robe down to the feet, with the folds turned back, and tucked under the belt. This belt, as we have ſaid, is of exquiſite workmanſhip, with bells attached to it, ſimilar to the inſtruments mentioned above, and ſo arranged that when fighting with their enemies the ſounds give them courage. Their buſkins are the ſame as thoſe worn by the Portugueſe. We have already ſpoken of their weapons, which conſiſt of bows, arrows, ſwords, daggers, and targets; theſe are diſtributed in ſuch manner that he who has a bow carries alſo a dagger, but not a target, theſe two laſt not being ſuitable to carry together, but only the ſword and ſhield. The common ſoldiers wear nothing above the waiſt, and for the reſt have bows, arrows, and daggers. Theſe firſt begin the ſkirmiſh attack, advancing in ſcattered groups, and provoke the enemy to fight, leaping quickly round from one ſide to another to avoid the enemies' blows. Young men alſo as has been ſaid, run ſwiftly in front, beating the drums, as if to encourage their comrades; and when it ſeems to the captain-general theſe are already weary, he recalls them by ſounding one of the inſtruments. When thus withdrawn from the combat they wheel round, and are ſucceeded by others in the fight, ſo that the army in this manner brings all the forces to bear in fighting the battle out.

In this battle various aſſaults were made by the contending armies, and in the firſt encounters the Congo people were victorious; but afterwards, both ſides having ſuffered great loſs, and as from lack of ſupplies the men were ill and dying, the camp of the King of Congo was broken up, and all returned home. Paulo Diaz being thus unable to join his allies, went forward, and croſſing the river entrenched himſelf in Luiola, a ſtrong natural poſition, where he could reſiſt the King of Angola. Luiola is thus ſtrong becauſe the Rivers Coanza and Luiola joining 105 miles from the coaſt, and approaching each other again within a bow-ſhot a little above their confluence, make a ſort of iſland between them. In this iſland, at the meeting of the two rivers, a hill riſes, which was taken by Paulo Diaz, and, to make it more ſecure, fortified. Formerly it was not inhabited, but has now become a ſmall country, peopled by the Portugueſe. From Luiola the river is navigated as far as the ſea in ſmall boats; and one can go, without riſk, for 105 miles by land. Near it are the Cabambe Mountains, producing much ſilver, which the ſaid Diaz was always trying to ſecure for himſelf. And it was on account of theſe mountains that the quarrel between himſelf and the people of Angola took place, for the latter, knowing the Portugueſe ſet great value on the mountains, becauſe of their ſilver mines, did all they could to prevent them coming there. They fought againſt each other, alſo, in other parts, for as the Portugueſe navigated the River Coanza they were continually making inroads into the countries ſubject to the King of Angola. The weapons uſed by this people are bows, ſix ſpans long, with ſtrings made of the bark of trees, and arrows of light wood, leſs than a man's little finger, alſo ſix ſpans in length, with iron heads made like a hook, and feathers of birds on the top. Of theſe they carry ſix or ſeven in the ſame hand with the bow, and without any quiver. The handle of their daggers reſembles that of a knife; and theſe they carry in the left ſide of the belt, and uſe with the hand uppermoſt. In military movements they uſe the ſtratagems of war and its various manœuvres, for when fighting againſt the Portugueſe it was ſeen they knew their advantage over the enemy, attacking them at night, or during rainy weather, when the guns and bombs would not take fire, and dividing their forces into ſeveral troops. The king does not go to war in perſon, but ſends his captains. Theſe people flee directly they ſee their captain ſlain, and no argument can ſtop them, from giving up the advantage. They are all infantry ſoldiers, and have no cavalry. The captains, when not wiſhing to walk, are carried by ſlaves in one of three manners, of which we ſhall ſpeak hereafter. Theſe people go to battle in great numbers, and in great diſorder, no one remaining behind who is at all fit for action. They make no ſuch proviſion as is neceſſary for a camp, and thoſe who do take any victuals have them carried on the ſhoulders of their ſlaves. Neverthelеſs, there are many animals which they could domeſticate and adapt for drawing and carrying, and about which we ſhall ſpeak in another part of this hiſtory. Thus it comes to paſs that arriving at a certain place, with the whole army, their proviſions conſumed, and nothing left for food, and juſt when the need of the expedition is at its height, they are obliged to return to their own country, being overcome with famine.

Theſe people are very ſuperſtitious, and if a bird chance to fly on their left hand, or cries in a certain manner, which they profeſs to underſtand predicts danger or ill-luck, or that they are to proceed no farther, they turn back at once, a cuſtom alſo obſerved by the Romans in early times, and by other heathen nations at this day. And if it appears ſtrange that the few Portugueſe ſoldiers who followed Paulo Diaz, with others of the ſame nation who traded in that kingdom, and gave him aid to the number of 300 at the moſt, and who, together with their ſlaves, and the malcontents and fugitives who fled from Angola to join him, and at no time exceeding the number of 15 thousand men, could poſſibly make ſuch gallant reſiſtance to theſe innumerable hoſts of negroes, amounting, it is ſaid, to a million of ſouls, and ſubjects of the King of Angola, I reply, that might eaſily happen, ſeeing that the negroes wore no clothing, neither had they any defenſive weapons, and their offenſive ones, conſiſting only of bows and daggers, as has been ſaid; whereas our ſmall numbers were well covered with quilted jerkins, lined with cotton, double-ſewn, which protected them from the arms down to the knees, their heads being covered with caps of this ſame material, which was proof againſt arrows and daggers. Beſides this, they uſed long ſwords, ſome of their cavalry carrying ſpears. One cavalry ſoldier is equal to a hundred negroes, who are greatly afraid of horſemen, and, above all, of thoſe who fire the guns and pieces of artillery, which cauſe them extreme terror. So that the few, if well-armed and ſkilfully diſpoſed, eaſily conquer the larger hoſts.

This Kingdom of Angola is populated to an incredible extent, the men taking as many wives as they wiſh, and the people multiplying without end, which is not the caſe in Congo, for there they live as Chriſtians. So that as Duarte Lopez ſaid, and believed, the Kingdom of Angola has nearly a million fighting-men, for every man having many wives, ſo alſo many ſons are born to them, and all go willingly to battle in the ſervice of their prince.

The country is peculiarly rich in mines of ſilver and copper, and there is a greater abundance of various metals than in any other country in the world. It alſo abounds in all manner of produce, has various animals, and, particularly, herds of cows. It is a fact that theſe people prefer dog's fleſh to any other food, and the animals are fattened on that account, and cut in pieces and ſold in the public ſhambles. It is aſſerted that a very large dog, reſembling a bull, is ſold in exchange for 22 ſlaves, which at 10 ducats a head, would coſt 220 ducats; ſo greatly are theſe animals prized. The money uſed in Angola differs from the Lumache of Congo, for it conſiſts of glaſs beads, the size of a nut, and ſmaller, of various forms and colours, which are made in Venice. Theſe are uſed not only as money, but for ornaments, both by men and women, who wear them on the neck and arms, and are called in their tongue, Anzolos, but when threaded in the form of a roſary, Mizanga.

The King of Angola is a pagan, worſhipping idols, like all his people. It is true he wiſhed to become a Chriſtian, after the example of the King of Congo, but as up to this time it has been found impoſſible to ſend prieſts to inſtruct him, he has remained in darkneſs. The above-named Duarte Lopez records, that in his time this king ſent ambaſſadors to the King of Congo, aſking for prieſts to inſtruct him in the Chriſtian faith, but, there being none with him, he was unable to do ſo. Theſe two kings have now made a treaty of peace, the Angola ruler being forgiven the attack and carnage committed by him on the people of Congo, and on the Portugueſe, at Cabazo.

The language of Angola is the ſame as that of Congo, for, as we have ſaid, it is all one kingdom, the only difference being ſuch as is frequently ſeen between neighbouring countries. For between Portugueſe and Caſtilians, or between Venetians and Calabrians, the dialects are ſo various, and the words twiſted into ſuch different forms (although all have the ſame idiom), that it is with difficulty they underſtand one another.

We have ſaid that il Seno delle Vacche divides the Kingdom of Angola in the middle, one half of which only has been referred to. Now we ſhall deſcribe the ſecond half, which extends from il Seno delle Vacche to the ſouth. From il Seno delle Vacche to the cape called Black Cape (Cape Negro), by way of the coaſt, extends 200 miles of country ſimilar to that deſcribed above, and is the territory of lords ſubject to the King of Angola. A line drawn towards the eaſt from Black Cape cuts through the mountains called Monti Freddi, which in certain parts, higher up towards the equinoctial line, are known as Monti Nevoſi, to the Portugueſe, and this line ends at the baſe of other mountains, called del Criſtallo. From theſe Monti Nevoſi come the waters of Lake Dumbea Zocche. The above line extends from Montagna del Criſtallo northward, through the Monte del Argento, as far as Malomba, where, as we have ſaid, the Kingdom of Congo is divided, the River Coari parting in the middle. Such is the kingdom ruled over by the King of Angola, of which we have nothing more to ſay, nor anything relating to the king himſelf or his Court.

CHAPTER VIII.

OF THE EXTENT OF THE KINGDOM OF CONGO IN POSSESSION OF THE REIGNING KING, ACCORDING TO THE ABOVE FOUR DIVISIONS.

STARTING from the Coanza River, and traverſing a diſtance of 375 miles towards the equinoctial line, we find the river called las Bareras vermeglias, for the ruins of certain rocks worn by the ſea falling into it give it that colour. From thence, in a direct line, the king has 450 miles of territory, and this line, going onwards towards the ſouth, paſſes the Mountains del Criſtallo (which are not thoſe of Angola, already referred to, but others), and the Mountains del Salnitro, and, croſſing the River Verbela, at the foot of the Mountains del Argento, terminates, at a diſtance of 500 miles, in the Lake of Achelunda. The fourth line takes the courſe of the River Coanza, which flows from the ſaid lake, a diſtance of 360 miles, ſo that the entire extent of the kingdom at preſent ruled over by King Don Alvarez of Congo meaſures 1685 miles. But the way for croſſing over this country commences at the mouth of the River Zaire, at the point known to the Portugueſe as Padraon, and cutting right through the Kingdom of Congo, and croſſing the Sun and Cryſtal Mountains, ends at a diſtance of 600 miles, and 150 miles from the Nile. It is true that formerly the anceſtors of this prince ruled over many neighbouring countries, which, in proceſs of time they loſt, though they ſtill retain the titles of all thoſe regions now governed by others, as, for example, Don Alvarez, King of Congo, and of Abundos, and of Matama, and of Quizama, and of Angola, and of Angoi, and of Cacongo, and of the ſeven Kingdoms of Congere

Amolaza, and of the Pangelungos, and Lord of the River Zaire, and of the Anziquos, and of Anziquana, and of Loanga, &c.

Provinces of the Kingdom of Congo.

This kingdom is divided into ſix provinces, called Bamba, Sogno, Sundi, Pango, Batta, and Pemba. That of Bamba, which is the largeſt and richeſt, is governed by Don Sebaſtian Manibamba, couſin of King Don Alvarez, lately deceaſed, and is ſituated by the ſea-coaſt, reaching from the River Ambize to that of Coanza on the ſouth. This prince has many lords under him, the names of the principal being Don Antonio Mani Bamba, who is lieutenant and brother of Don Sebaſtian, and another, Mani Lemba, and Mani Dandi, Mani Bengo, and Mani Loanda, Governor of the Iſland of Loanda; and Mani Corimba, Mani Coanza, and Mani Cazzanzi. All theſe govern the ſea coaſt line; but in the interior, where the land belongs to Angola, the Ambundos are made rulers, who, living on the borders of Angola, are alſo ſubject to the ſame Manibamba, and are the Angazi, Chinchengo, Motollo, Chabonda, and many others of lower rank. Note that this word Mani means Lord, the ſecond half referring to the country and government under his rule; as for example, Mani Bamba means lord of the country of Bamba, and Mani Corimba, which is part of Bamba, lord of Corimba, and ſo with the reſt. This Province of Bamba is bounded by Angola on the ſouth, and on the eaſt, towards the Lake Achelunda, lies Chezzama, a country which is under a republic, and divided into many lordſhips, the people not being in ſubjection to the King of Congo, nor, indeed, to the King of Angola. Ultimately, after having greatly reſiſted Paulo Diaz, theſe Chizzama lords became ſubject to him, in order to eſcape the yoke of the King of Angola; and Diaz made uſe of them himſelf againſt the ſaid king. Now, this country of Bamba, as has been ſaid, is the principal one in the Kingdom of Congo; its key, buckler, ſword, and defence, and the barrier againſt its enemies. So that it is able to reſiſt every rebellion in thoſe parts, having brave people always ready for war, reſiſting its Angola enemies, and helping the king in quelling diſturbances cauſed by other countries. When neceſſary, they can bring into the field four hundred thouſand armed men, although that is only the ſixth part of the kingdom, but the beſt and largeſt. The principal city of this province lies in the plain between the Rivers Loze and Ambrize, and is called Panza, a name common to every territory. The governor lives here, and it is a hundred miles from the ſea. In this province, the mountains, ſtretching out to the Angola Kingdom, firſt begin to appear, where ſilver mines, and thoſe of all other metals are found. It is very rich, for along its ſea-ſhores are found the Lumache which ſerve as money in the Congo kingdom. Here alſo is the largeſt traffic in ſlaves, who are brought from Angola, for they buy from the Portugueſe every year more than five thouſand negroes, and then take them to various parts for ſale. The people of this province are the braveſt in the whole kingdom, and are armed with long and large ſwords, like thoſe of the Slavonians, which are brought them from Portugal. Mighty men alſo are amongſt them, who at one blow cut a ſlave through the middle, and take off the head of a bull with the ſtroke of one of theſe ſwords, and more than this (a thing which ſeems incredible), one of theſe valiant men can hold on his arm a veſſel containing the fourth part of a butt of wine until the veſſel has emptied itſelf. They uſe bows and arrows with great ſkill and dexterity; and beſides theſe weapons they have long ſhields, made of Dant's ſkin, of which we have already ſpoken, as uſed by the Anzichi.

Animals found in the Province of Pamba.

The animals found in this region are, firſt, elephants, which abound in all the Congo kingdom, but chiefly in Pamba, on account of foreſts, paſtures, and water being more abundant there than in any other part of that country, ſo many rivers flowing through it, and thus furniſhing food for theſe enormous creatures. Lopez ſaid he had often meaſured the ſize of an elephant's foot in the duſt of four ſpans in width, from which one can (by making a circle) gueſs the ſize of the whole body of this beaſt. The foot is called malo manzao, that is, foot of an elephant. When in our time, in Portugal, Italy, or Germany, theſe animals are found much ſmaller in ſize than thoſe we have referred to, it is becauſe they are young ones, and were taken to thoſe countries at an early age, in order to domeſticate them. They are reckoned in theſe regions to live 150 years, and only ceaſe growing at middle age. In ſupport of this ſtatement Lopez added that he had ſeen teeth, not of horn, as ſome think, which weighed 200 pounds 12 ounces. In the Congo tongue they are called Mene Manzao, or tooth of the elephant. The young elephant is known as Moana Manzao, or ſon of the elephant. Their ears are bigger than the largeſt Turkiſh ſhields, being ſix ſpans long, and egg-ſhaped, and narrower and more pointed towards the ſhoulders; and with them they chaſe away flies, as well as with their trunk and tail. It is ſaid, that when they cannot reach the offenders with theſe they curl up their ſkin, and ſo kill them.

In their tails are long ſilken hairs, ſprinkled with black and ſhining ones, thoſe in the older animals being ſtrongeſt and fineſt, and moſt highly prized by theſe people, both noble men and women in Angola, and in the adjoining country of Ambundo, uſing them as ornaments for the neck, and eſteeming them not only for their beauty, but as the produce of theſe large animals. They are very thick, like a rope, and cannot be pulled apart with all the ſtrength poſſible, the hands being injured even in the attempt. To procure them many lie in wait for the elephants as they aſcend narrow and ſteep paths, going behind them, and with ſharp knives cutting off their tails. One ſuch tail is equal in value to two or three ſlaves. The beaſts cannot turn to revenge themſelves in theſe narrow defiles, nor can they reach their enemies with their trunks. Some, who are agile and brave, attack the elephants by ſtealth from behind, whilſt they are feeding, and try, with one blow, to cut off the tail, ſaving themſelves by running round and round, for, notwithſtanding the ſize of theſe creatures, they run very ſwiftly in a ſtraight line, and take long ſteps, though ſlow ones. In an open plain they are ſwifter than the fleeteſt horſe, but when turning they loſe time, and ſo the hunter eſcapes. Many, however, are caught and killed by the elephants when purſued by them on a ſtraight road.

The ancients, who were ill-informed on the ſubject, aſſert that elephants could not lie down, but leant upon trees, which, when ſawn down by hunters, the elephants fell with them, and being thus rendered helpleſs were caught as they lay on the ground. But Duarte Lopez ſays that they not only lie down, but alſo kneel, and leap with their forefeet on trees to feed on leaves, and ſtoop to drink water, which is often found in their caves. Their joints reſemble thoſe of other animals, although differing in ſome reſpects, for from the fore feet to the ſhoulders they have only two joints. Whilſt feeding they root up large trees with their ſhoulders and back, but take ſmaller trees between their teeth, twiſting and dragging them, in order to feed on the leaves. Sometimes it happens that one of their teeth is broken, and thus many are found ſcattered over the open plains who have loſt their teeth. They eat with ſhort teeth, which are not ſeen as the two long tuſks are, and take their food into the mouth with their trunk, as if it were a hand and arm, the end of which is formed like a finger; with this they can take up the ſmalleſt things, ſuch as nuts, ſtraw, and wheat, and put them into the mouth, as I, Filippo, have ſeen myſelf at Liſbon.

As the young elephant cannot be reared quickly, being ſlow of growth, the milk is kept from it, and it ſoon learns to feed itſelf. Mother nature has ſo provided that only once in ſeven years theſe animals bring forth their young. Their ſkin is hard beyond belief, being four fingers thick, and impoſſible to pierce, even with a gun. Lopez records that with a ſmall gun, called a Petreraa, he hit one without wounding it, but it was badly bruised, and went three days' journey in a dying condition, when meeting ſome ſlaves by the way, in its maddened ſtate, it threw them down and killed them. The natives do not know how to tame theſe animals, of whom ſo much uſe might be made in tranſporting merchandize, and in many other ways. They are captured by drawing them into deep trenches in parts where they are accuſtomed to feed. Theſe trenches are narrow at the bottom, and larger above, ſo that the animals cannot help themſelves, and when leaping forward, fall down again. Earth, graſs, and leaves are covered over theſe trenches, which act as a blind, and the animals paſſing over them fall into the trap. Lopez ſaid he had, with his own eyes, ſeen a very wonderful thing in Coanza, for a young elephant, following its mother, having fallen into a pit, from which ſhe failed to draw it out, though uſing all the ſtrength poſſible for its reſcue; whereupon ſhe buried it therein, and covered it with graſs, branches, and young ſhoots of trees, filling up the hole, ſo that the hunters ſhould not have the ſatiſfaction of its capture, preferring rather to kill it than allow it to fall into their hands. This tender mother, not fearing the crowd who ſtood around with various weapons, and angry ſounds directed againſt her, confident in her own ſtrong nature was unwearying from morning till night in trying to drive them back, and failing to do ſo acted as we have related. The elephant is a gentle beaſt, and, truſting in its great ſtrength, has no fear, doing injury to none when unmoleſted, and approaching dwellings without any ſign of ill-will. They do not attack, unleſs interfered with, only ſometimes they will gently hoiſt with their trunk into the air any one they may meet by the way. They delight in water, and may beſt be ſeen by the rivers and lakes, where it is their habit at noontide to go and drink and refreſh themſelves, bathing and ſtanding up to their middle in water, and throwing over the reſt of the body great quantities of water by means of their trunk. On account of the large paſtures and number of fords in the Kingdom of Congo great numbers of theſe creatures are found there. Duarte Lopez ſays he has ſeen them paſs from Cazanze to Loanda through a ſmall graſſy valley to the number of 100 (going in companies, like cows, camels, and ſuchlike animals, and not alone, like lions, and other wild beaſts), large and ſmall, the latter following the mothers, and being the firſt young ones he had ſeen. Abundance of ivory being found here, muſt be the produce of the great number of elephants; and beſides, ivory was not accounted valuable till after the Portugueſe begun to trade in theſe regions. As it muſt have accumulated to a great extent for centuries, it is, even to this day, to be had for a ſmall price.

It is not known if there are any other animals as large as the elephant in theſe countries, nor if the rhinoceros, ſimilar to it, and called Bada in India, exiſts here. But it is well known that the horns which grow on the noſe of that beaſt are brought to the country of the Anzichi, and greatly prized there, being uſed for divers maladies, ſo that it is poſſible ſome may be found in theſe parts. The lions in the Anzichi country are ſimilar to thoſe found in different parts of the world, but they are not ſeen in Bamba, where, however, tigers of the very ſame form as thoſe ſeen by Duarte Lopez at Florence are found in great numbers, who teſtified to their being really tigers. He told alſo of a curious habit amongſt them, which is, that they do not moleſt white men, but only black ones, and even kill and eat black men whilſt aſleep, ſparing white ones. If unable to ſatiſfy their hunger in the open country, they fearleſſly drag from the very courts of the houſes any animals they find there, ſparing none. In the Congo tongue they are called Engoi. Theſe beaſts are as fierce as lions, roaring in the ſame manner, and reſembling them in all reſpects, except the ſkin, that of the tiger being ſpotted, whereas the lion is all of one colour. Tigers are caught and killed in various ways, poiſon being ſometimes mixed with their food. Snares alſo are laid, in which a kid is placed, and when the hungry beaſt ſeeks for prey he is ſuddenly caught in one of theſe ſnares, and, trying to releaſe himſelf, becomes more and more entangled, and ſo is ſecured. Another mode of capture is to attack him with arrows, ſpears, and fire-arms. The tiger is an enemy to the negro, to ſheep-folds, and even to cattle. Notwithſtanding, Duarte Lopez tells of one reared by himſelf from 15 days old, and fed on goat's milk. When full-grown it followed him like a dog, being quite tame, but allowed no one to touch it but its maſter. Nevertheleſs, this creature roared, and its eyes glared fearfully. In proceſs of time it killed a favourite dog, and alſo a pet

Zebra belonging to its maſter, who, ſeeing the tiger was a dangerous animal, ſhot him. He adds that in this region the whiſkers of the tiger are conſidered deadly poiſon, and when given in food cauſe death, as if from madneſs. Therefore, whoever brings a ſkin of this animal without the whiſkers, the king cauſes to be puniſhed.

In this country another animal is found, called the Zebra. It is common alſo to ſome parts of Barbary and Africa, and, though in all reſpects like a mule, ſtill is not one, as it produces male progeny. It has a very peculiar ſkin, and different from all other creatures, inaſmuch as from the back bone round towards the body it is ſtreaked with three colours, black, white, and dark brown. Theſe large ſtripes are three fingers' length from each other, and meet in a circle, every row with its own colour. The neck and head are marked in the ſame manner, as well as the ears and legs; ſo that a ſtreak beginning with white is invariably followed by black, and then by dark brown, always maintaining the ſame regularity of colour. The mane is not long. The tail, like that of the mule, is very gloſſy, and of good colour. The feet and hoofs are alſo like thoſe of the mule. This animal reſembles the horſe in its fleetneſs, for ſo rapid is its motion that, in Portugal and Caſtile, they ſtill ſay, as ſwift as a zebra, to denote extreme ſpeed. Theſe animals bring forth their young every year, and are found in large numbers quite wild. When tamed, they are uſed for riding, for tranſport ſervice, and alſo as good war-horſes, as well as in many other ways. From all this we ſee that mother nature has provided in every country for the convenience and neceſſities of man a variety of animals, of food, and of climate, ſo that nothing is lacking for his comfort. Not having, however, horſes in any part of the Kingdom of Congo, nor knowing how to train oxen to the yoke or the pack ſaddle, for drawing or carrying, neither how to tame zebras with bridle and ſaddle, or, indeed, in any way to transport their merchandise from place to place by means of theſe animals, they are of neceſſity obliged to employ men inſtead of beaſts of burden. And ſo, lying down in a ſort of litter, or ſeated in them, and protected from the ſun with umbrellas, the people are carried by their ſlaves, or elſe by men who are ſtationed at various poſts for hire. Whoever wiſhes to travel quickly muſt take many ſlaves with him, and when the firſt carriers are tired a ſecond ſet take up the load, ſo changing continually, in the ſame way as the Tartars and the Perſians do with their horſes. Theſe men travel very rapidly, being accuſtomed to their burdens, and, by conſtant changing rival a poſtillion's gallop. Of the manner in which theſe people are carried, whilſt travelling, we have furniſhed pictures, and alſo of the zebra, of the dreſs of men and women, of ſoldiers, of military inſtruments, and of the palm-tree.

Other animals are found in theſe regions ſtanding about four feet leſs than oxen, with red-coloured ſkins, and horns like a goat, black, ſmooth, and gliſtening, of which they make pretty ornaments, ſuch as are made alſo from buffalo horns. Their heads and hair reſemble thoſe of the ox, and their ſkins are much prized, being taken to Portugal, and from thence to Germany to be dreſſed, and are called Dants. The King of Congo was deſirous of having workmen ſkilled in the art of dreſſing and cleanſing theſe ſkins, ſo as to make them into weapons of defence. Neverthleſs, theſe people uſe them as ſhields and targets againſt the blows of different weapons, and eſpecially againſt arrows. Theſe animals are killed both with guns and arrows, but if they eſpy the hunter they attack him, and, being fierce and courageous, will injure him with their feet and muzzle, not being able to do ſo with their horns, and leave him almoſt, or indeed altogether dead. Innumerable herds of wild buffaloes, wander about the deſerts of the Anzicana Kingdom, as well as numbers of wild aſſes, which the Greeks call Onagri. Beſides theſe, one finds alſo other beaſts called Empalanga, which reſemble the ox in bigneſs and form, except that they hold the head and neck aloft. Their horns are broad and crooked, three ſpans long, and divided into knots, but ſharp at the points; and from theſe fine ſounding horns are made. Although theſe creatures live in the foreſts they are quite harmleſs. The ſkins of their necks are uſed for ſhoe ſoles, and their fleſh for food. They might be taught to draw the plough, and alſo ſerve in various ways for huſbandry. Large herds of kine and tame oxen feed here. There are alſo pigs, wild boars, and flocks of ſheep and goats. Theſe ſheep and goats, Don Lopez ſays, bring forth two, three, or four lambs, or kids, at a time, but never only one. On account of the paſtures being ſo rich theſe animals are all brought up by their own dams, and Lopez proved this to be the caſe, as he had ſeveral head of them in his own dwellings.

Wolves, too, live in theſe regions, who are beyond meaſure fond of palm oil, and ſcent it afar off, as they poſſeſs the ſame ſenſe of ſmell which Virgil attributes to dogs, odora canum vis. The oil, as has been ſaid, is made from the palm-tree, and is thick and hard like butter; and it is wonderful how theſe wolves can take a gourd full of it between their teeth and carry it away on their ſhoulders, in the ſame way as wolves carry off ſheep with us. Foxes abound here, which alſo, like thoſe in our own parts, ſteal poultry. In this Province of Pamba there are innumerable animals for the chaſe, such as ſtags, fallow deer, roebuck, and gazelles, of which laſt Lopez ſaid he had ſeen great herds, and alſo numbers of rabbits and hares, there being no hunters to kill them.

In this ſame province are many wild civet cats, called by the Portugueſe Algazia, and ſome had been tamed by the people of the country for the ſake of their perfume, in which they greatly delight. This was before the Portugueſe traded in thoſe parts. In Manibatta a great number of ſables are caught, which have exceedingly fine grey hairs. They are called Incire, and no one is allowed to uſe the ſkins of theſe creatures except by permiſſion of the prince of the province, their value being ſuch that one ſkin is equal to the price of a ſlave. Towards the Anzicana region martens alſo are caught, and their ſkins made into garments, to which we ſhall refer in due time.

Apes, monkeys, and ſimilar animals of every deſcription, both large and ſmall, are found in the country of Songo, which lies by the River Zaire. Some of theſe creatures are very amuſing, and are kept by the Lords in thoſe parts for paſtime, but eſpecially for ſport; and although without reaſoning powers, yet they imitate to a great extent the actions and manners of mankind. In all the above-named regions theſe different animals are found in greater or leſſer numbers.

The ſnakes and ſerpents here are of an entirely different ſpecies from thoſe of our own countries, being enormous and frightful in form, and ſome meaſuring 25 ſpans long, and 5 broad. The ſtomach and mouth of theſe creatures are ſo large that they can ſwallow a ſtag, or any other animal of equal ſize. They are called * * * * * * * * *, that is, a large waterſnake, which comes on land to feed, and then returns to the river, living in both elements alike. They cling to the branches of trees, and lying in wait for animals who come to feed near, when they are ſufficiently cloſe that they can drop on to them they wriggle down, and catching the animal by the tail, cruſh and ſtrangle it to death, after which they drag it to ſome ſolitary wood, or other ſpot, where they ſlowly devour it, even to the ſkin, the horns, and the claws. Now, when thus gorged they remain in a ſtate of torpor, and might be killed by a child, being ſatiſfied with this food for five or ſix days, and then again ſeek for prey. They change their ſkins at certain ſeaſons, and even ſometimes after having eaten largely, which ſkins are found afterwards and collected as ſpecimens of the ſize of theſe creatures. This ſnake is much prized as food by the heathen natives, even more ſo than fowls and like delicate flesh, and they eat it roaſted, finding great numbers of them lying burnt on the ground, when they ſet fire to their thick woods.

Beſides theſe there are vipers, well known to be ſo poiſonous that any one bitten by them dies in 24 hours, yet the negroes know of a certain herb which heals their wounds. There are certain other creatures about the ſize of a ram, which have wings and tails like dragons, and a long ſnout, with divers rows of teeth, and which eat raw fleſh. Their colour is azure blue and green, their ſkin having the appearance of ſcales, and they are two-footed creatures. The pagan natives worſhip them as gods, and to this day ſome are preſerved as wonders by theſe people. To make them ſtill more valued, the nobles have them in their own keeping, in order to obtain from thoſe who come to worſhip them gifts and oblations. Four-footed chameleons are found here on the rocks, about the ſize of lizards and ſuch-like creatures, with pointed heads, and tails like a ſaw. They are moſtly of dark bluiſh and greeniſh colours, and even whilſt looking at them one ſees their colours change rapidly. They live chiefly on high rocks and trees, to breathe the air, with which they are nouriſhed. Other venomous ſerpents found here carry at the end of their tails a ſort of ball, like a bell, which rings as if nature had placed it there to warn thoſe who were approaching to beware of danger. Theſe bells and the heads of the ſerpents are remedies for fever and palpitation of the heart. Such are the kind of creatures found in theſe regions, with others alſo common to other countries.

It remains now to ſpeak of the Birds, and firſt of Oſtriches, as being larger than any other. Theſe are found in thoſe parts of Sundi and of Batta bordering on the Muzombi, the young ones iſſuing from an egg warmed by the ſun. Their feathers are uſed as ſtandards and banners in battle, and are mixed with thoſe of the peacock in the form of a ſun umbrella. And as we are talking of peacocks I may ſay that in theſe parts of Angola peacocks are reared in a wood ſurrounded by walls, the king not permitting any one to have theſe birds but himſelf, on account of the royal ſtandards above mentioned. One reads in the ancient hiſtories of Alexander the Great, that this bird was as highly prized when it was firſt ſeen in Europe. Here alſo are the cocks called Indian ones, and hens, geeſe, and ducks of every kind, both wild and tame, and partridges in ſuch numbers that children can catch them with a nooſe. There are alſo other birds like pheaſants, called Gallignoles, doves, pigeons, and great numbers of thoſe birds called fig-peckers. Birds of prey, ſuch as Royal eagles, falcons, goſhawks, ſparrow-hawks, and others found here are not uſed for hawking. Sea-birds, ſuch as large and white Pelicans, ſo called by the Portugueſe, ſwim under the water, whoſe throats are ſo large that they ſwallow a fiſh whole, and whoſe ſtomachs are ſo ſtrong, and ſo hot by nature, that they eaſily digeſt fiſhes entire. Their ſkins are ſo warm that the people of the country uſe them as covering, and prize them greatly. Great numbers of white herons and grey bitterns, called royal birds, feed here in the fords. There are certain birds alſo, reſembling cranes with red beaks, red legs, and as large as ſwans; their feathers are for the moſt part red, the reſt white, and ſome have dark-coloured creſts. Theſe birds, called by the people of the country Flamingoes, which they reſemble, are very beautiful; and are alſo uſed for food.

Large grey parrots, which are good talkers, abound here, as well as ſmall green ones, which do not talk much. There are certain ſmall birds, too, called birds of muſic, larger than canaries, with red feathers and beaks, others being green, with black feet and bill. Some are all white, others grey, or all black. Theſe laſt ſing more beautifully than the reſt, and ſeem almoſt to ſpeak in their ſongs. There are others which ſing in various ways, but all ſo ſweetly that the lords of this country have for centuries kept ſuch birds in cages, and prized them highly for their ſong.

CHAPTER IX.

OF THE PROVINCE OF SONGO, WHICH IS THE COUNTRY OF THE RIVER ZAIRE, AND OF LOANGO.

THIS province is bounded ſeven and a half degrees north by the River Ambrize, and, after croſſing the Rivers Lelunda and Zaire, its confines terminate at the Red Rocks, which are on the borders of the Kingdom of Loango. In the centre of this province is a territory of the ſame name, called Songo, where the governor of the country lives. The lords ruling this country are called Mani Songo, or Lords of Songo, and are uſually of the blood royal. He who now reigns is Don Diego Mani Songo, and under him are ſeveral leſſer lords and provinces, which in old time were free, like the people of Mombalas, living nearer the City of Congo, but who are now under this government. On the other ſide of the River Zaire, towards the north, is the Province of Palmar, ſo called from the number of palm-trees growing there. Other lordſhips border on the territory of the King of Loango, who formerly was ſubject to the King of Congo, but in proceſs of time became independent, and now profeſſes to be a friend of that king, but not a vaſſal. The people of this country were called Bramas in former days, and lived inland eaſtward, under the equinoctial line, as far as the borders of Anzicana, all along the mountains which divide them from the Anzichi on the north. Theſe Anzichi are called Congreamolal by the people of Loango, becauſe they were formerly ſubject to Congo.

Many elephants are found in Loango, and alſo much ivory. Ivory they exchange for iron, and even a nail from a ſhip is taken in exchange for a whole elephant's tooth. This muſt be either becauſe no iron is found here, or the working of it is unknown. Theſe people uſe it as points for arrows, and for other weapons, as we have ſaid before, when ſpeaking of the Bramas. They make alſo cloths from the palm-tree, ſuch as we have ſpoken of above, but ſmaller and finer ones. Cows and other animals of the kind abound.

The people are pagans, and their dreſs is like that uſed in Congo. They go to war with their neighbouring enemies, who are the natives of Anzicana; and when fighting againſt them they aſk help from Congo, thus preſerving themſelves partly independent. They worſhip what they pleaſe, their chief deity being the ſun, as repreſenting the male, and the moon as the female. For the reſt each chooſes his own idol, which he worſhips according to pleaſure. Theſe people

I

would gladly embrace the Chriſtian faith, as many of them who live on the confines of Congo are already converted to it, and the reſt, only from lack of prieſts and of others to teach them the true doctrine, remain in error.

CHAPTER X.

OF THE THIRD PROVINCE, CALLED SUNDI.

THIS Province of Sundi is the one neareſt to the City of Congo, called San Salvador, although quite beyond that territory, and 40 miles diſtant from it. It extends to the River Zaire, and over the ſame to the other ſide as far as the Caduta, or Fall, of which we have ſpoken above. It ſtretches along both ſides of the river, bordering on Anzicana northwards, and towards the ſouth extends along the ſaid river to its junction with the River Bancare, and along its banks as far as the foot of the Monte del Criſtallo. Its principal town is on the confines of the Province of Pango, where the governor of the province bearing the ſame name lives, that is to ſay, of Sundi ; and it lies a day's journey to the ſouth of the falls of the river. This province is the chief one, forming almoſt the patrimony of the whole Kingdom of Congo, and therefore always governed by the eldeſt ſon of the king and the princes who are firſt in ſucceſſion, as it came to paſſ in the time of the firſt Chriſtian king, Don Juan, whoſe eldeſt ſon, Don Alfonſo, having previouſly been governor here, ſucceeded his father. All ſucceſſive kings have obſerved the ſame cuſtom, giving the government to the princes who were next in ſeniority, and in the ſame way the preſent King Don Alvarez was himſelf formerly governor, and called Mani Sundi. It muſt be obſerved here that in the Kingdom of Congo, no one having property can leave it to his heirs. Everything belongs to the king, and he divides the government, riches, and territory to whomſoever he pleaſes, his own ſons being ſubject to the ſame law. In conſequence of which law, if any one omits to pay tribute every year, the king takes away their governorſhip giving it to another, as happened to the king who now reigns, at the time when Duarte Lopez was at this court; for wiſhing, when governor, to be liberal, and even boundleſs in generoſity to his vaſſals, who were diſſatiſfied with the burdens put upon them, he was for this diſobedience removed from his governorſhip and from the king's favour, which laſt is known in the language of this people as Tambocado, to which we ſhall allude fully in other parts of this book. A great number of Lords are under the rule of the Governor of Sundi. The people trade with the countries adjoining, ſelling and bartering ſalt and different kinds of cloth brought from India and Portugal and uſing Lumache as currency. They receive in exchange cloths made from the palm, ivory, ſables, and belts made from the leaves of the palm, beautifully worked, and much valued in theſe parts. Great numbers of cryſtals are found, and alſo ſeveral metals; but iron is moſt valued, and from it the people make knives, fire-arms ſwords, and ſimilar inſtruments uſeful to mankind.

CHAPTER XI.

OF THE FOURTH PROVINCE, CALLED PANGO.

THE country of Pango was formerly an independent kingdom. On the north it is bounded by Sundi, on the ſouth by Batta, on the weſt by Congo, and on the eaſt by the Montagne del Sole. Its chief city, which is the reſidence of the governor, has the ſame name, and is ſituated on the weſt bank of the River Barbela. Originally it was called Pangelungos, which has in time been corrupted into Pango. The River Barbela runs through the middle of it, this river taking its riſe in the great lake from which the Nile flows, and alſo from a ſmaller lake, called Achelunda, and falling into the Zaire. Although the ſmalleſt province, nevertheleſs it does not yield leſs tribute. It was conquered after that of Sundi, and became ſubject to the princes of Congo, and now all have the ſame language and dreſs. The preſent governor is called Don Francesco Manipango, and belongs to the oldeſt nobility of the chiefs of Congo. In councils of ſtate he is always preſent, being already an old man and of great prudence; and for fifty years he has governed this kingdom without any outbreaks, or having once had to be recalled by the king. The trade of this province reſembles that of Sundi.

CHAPTER XII.

OF THE FIFTH PROVINCE, CALLED BATTA.

THIS country is bounded on the north by the Province of Pango, on the eaſt it croſſes the River Barbela, to the Monti del Sole and to the foot of the Salnitro range, and towards the ſouth of the ſaid mountains is bounded by a line paſſing from the junction of the Barbela and Cacinga Rivers to the Monte Bruciato. Within theſe limits lies Batta and its principal city, the reſidence of the governor, likewiſe called Batta. Formerly it was known as Aghirimba, afterwards the name was changed to Batta. The kingdom formerly was powerful and great, and voluntarily joined itſelf to that of Congo without any war, doubtleſs to avoid diſſenſions amongſt its chiefs, and has in conſequence greater advantages and freedom than any other province in the Congo Kingdom. The government of Batta is always therefore given to one of the blood royal of this country, according to the king's pleaſure, not having regard more to one than another, beyond keeping to the royal line. Neither the eldeſt nor the ſecond ſon inherit this poſt, but the King of Congo gives it, as we have ſaid, according to his pleasure, in order that there ſhall be neither uſurpation nor rebellion. This governor ranks nearer the king than any other in Congo, being ſecond perſon in the kingdom, nor can any one alter his decrees as they can thoſe of others, and on the failure of the royal line the ſucceſſion devolves upon him, and he is ſtyled Don Pedro Manibatta. Sometimes he eats at the king's table, but at a lower place, which is a privilege not granted to any other governor in Congo, nor even to the king's ſons. His court and attendants are little inferior to thoſe of the king himſelf, for when he goes abroad on any public occaſion he is preceded by trumpets, drums, and other martial inſtruments. He is commonly called Prince of Batta by the Portugueſe, becauſe, as has been ſaid, if the kings of Congo lacked heirs this kingdom would paſs to one of his blood. The neighbouring heathen tribes always go with him to battle, and he can bring into the field ſeventy or eighty thouſand men. As he is at continual warfare with the neighbouring tribes, he is allowed to have native fuſiliers, the king permitting no other governor, nor even his ſons, to employ native troops, but only Portugueſe ſoldiers. And Duarte Lopez having once aſked the king why he did not permit other governors to have thefe fufiliers, he replied that if there happened to be a rebellion amongft them, and they came againft him with one or two thoufand armed men, he would have no power to refift them. And as we have mentioned that the king only permits the ufe of native troops to the Prince of Batta it is right to add that it is neceffary for him to do this, as towards the eaft of Batta, beyond the Mountains del Sole and Salnitro, on the weft and eaftern fides of the Nile, and on the borders of the Kingdom of Moenhe Muge, live a people called Jaggas in Congo, but known in their own country by the name of Agag. They are a very favage and warlike people, much given to warfare and robbery, making conftant raids into the neighbouring countries, and fometimes into that of Batta, fo that it is not furprifing if the people of the latter country are conftantly on their guard, and keep armed foldiers, wherewith to defend themfelves. The Prince of Batta has many Lords under him, and the natives are called Monfobos, their language being underftood in Congo. They are a much ruder tribe than the Mociconghi, and flaves coming from them prove extremely obftinate. The trade is the fame as amongft the people of whom we have fpoken, but the revenue which the king draws from Batta amounts to double that of the two provinces above mentioned.

CHAPTER XIII.

OF THE SIXTH AND LAST PROVINCE, CALLED PEMBA.

THE Province of Pemba is fituated in the very centre of the Kingdom of Congo, being furrounded by, and comprifed within, the limits defcribed above. The governor is Don Antonio Manipemba, fecond fon of the late King Alvarez, and brother of the reigning fovereign. So much was Don Antonio beloved by his father that he affigned this governorfhip to him, not knowing what better to give, unlefs it were the royal kingdom itfelf, which he had defired to do, for he was more after his own heart than the eldeft fon; but this was not according to the royal law, and could not have been permitted. This province is the centre of the Kingdom of Congo, and the cradle of the ancient kingdoms, and in confequence of its being at the head of the other princedoms, the royal city is placed in its midft, of which we fhall later give full particulars.

The above-named Governor of Pemba lives in a territory of the fame name, fituated at the foot of the Monte Bruciato, and extending along the River Coze, which iffues from the lake and flows through the region of Bamba into the fea. The courtiers, Lords, and vaffals of the King of Congo have their riches and poffeffions in this province, in order to be near the court, and alfo as more convenient for conveying articles of food and clothing to the court. Some of thefe Lords, and particularly thofe in the parts bounded by Bamba, are obliged to fight againft and defend themfelves from their neareft neighbours, the people of Chizzama, who, it is faid, have revolted againft the King of Congo, and profefs to be independent.

Here we fhall conclude the Firft Book, which confifts in a general defcription of the Kingdom of Congo and its boundaries, and particularly of the provinces within it. It remains for us to proceed ftill farther in the Second, when we fhall treat of the fite of the City of Congo, and its territory; alfo of the prince to whofe baptifm the king came, and of his cuftoms and court, and other things pertaining to the civil and military government of theſe people. Later, we ſhall deſcribe the ſurrounding kingdoms and regions, reaching as far ſouth as the Cape of Good Hope, and even beyond the rivers and countries of the Indian Ocean; referring alſo to the interior of the country in which are the kingdoms of Preſter John, beſides touching on the ſources of the Nile and the reaſon of its wonderful overflow, which by the ignorant is regarded as miraculous.

BOOK THE SECOND.

CHAPTER I.

OF THE SITE OF THE ROYAL CITY OF THE KINGDOM OF CONGO.

ALTHOUGH the Royal City of the Kingdom of Congo is to a certain extent included in the region of Pemba, neverthelefs as the government thereof, and of its furrounding territory, which extends for about 20 miles, belongs to the king himfelf, let us treat of it feparately.

This city is called San Salvador, and was formerly known as Banza in the language of the country, which generally means Court, where the king or governor refides, and is fituated 150 miles from the fea, on a large and high mountain, almoft entirely of rock, in which neverthelefs is a feam of iron-ftone, of which large houfes are built. This mountain has on its fummit a plain, entirely cultivated, and furnifhed with hamlets and villages, extending for about ten miles in circumference, where more than 100,000 perfons are located. The land is fruitful, and the air healthy, and frefh, and pure, and there are fprings of moderately good water, but never injurious. Here, alfo, are many animals of every defcription. The fummit of the mountain is feparate, and diftinct from all others around it; and therefore the Portuguefe call it Oteiro, that is to fay, vedette, and fingular height, whence the whole country round can be feen. 'Tis true that only towards the eaſt and the river it is precipitous, and very craggy.

For two reaſons the earlieſt lords of the country placed this territory on the ſaid ſummit; firſt, becauſe it lies in almoſt the very middle of the kingdom, whence ſubſidies could be quickly ſent to every part; and, then, becauſe the natural elevation gives good air, a ſecure poſition, and one not to be taken by force. By the north-weſt aſcent, which looks towards the ſea, and which, as has been ſaid, is 150 miles off, the ſummit is reached by a five-miles' walk along a winding, broad, and well-made path. On the eaſt ſide a river runs along the baſe of the mountain, to which women deſcend, by a path a mile long, to waſh clothes. In ſome parts there are planted and cultivated valleys, nor is any region left without tillage, on account of its being the country where the Court reſides. The city is placed in a corner or angle of that ſummit, towards the ſouth-eaſt, and was encloſed with walls by King Dom Affonſo, the firſt Chriſtian, who gave the Portugueſe their own ſeparate part ſhut off with a wall, and encloſed his palace in the ſame way, as well as the other royal houſes. A large ſpace was left between theſe two encloſures, in which ſtands the principal church, with its ſquare in front, the gates of the houſes of the nobles and of the Portugueſe being built ſo as to face the ſaid church, and where the ſquare commences live certain great nobles of the Court. Behind the church, the ſquare ends in a narrow ſtreet, which has its own gate, outſide which are ſeveral houſes facing eaſt. Beyond theſe walls, in which the royal reſidences and the city of the Portugueſe are encloſed, there are ſeveral buildings belonging to nobles, every one taking the ſite moſt agreeable to him near the court. So that it is impoſſible to determine the ſize of this City, the whole country beyond the two boundaries of the walls being covered with houſes and palaces, each noble having his houſes and lands encloſed like a town. The Portugueſe occupy a circuit of nearly a mile, and other buildings, ſuch as the royal houſes, about the ſame extent. The walls are of great thickneſs; the gates are not ſhut at night, nor even are ſentinels poſted. There is no lack of water-ſprings on this high plain, but the Court and the Portugueſe drink from a continually-flowing fountain, on the north ſide, to which they deſcend the diſtance of a gunſhot down hill, and carry the water into the city in veſſels of wood and terra cotta, and alſo in gourds on the ſhoulders of ſlaves. The whole plain is fruitful and cultivated, having verdant meadows and large trees, and produces grain of various kinds. The beſt grain is called Luco, which is like muſtard ſeed, but larger. This is ground in a handmill, and from the white flour excellent bread is made, and ſuch as is not even inferior to corn, although only the latter is uſed in the celebration of maſs.

Theſe different kinds of grain have been plentiful throughout the Kingdom of Congo for a little while paſt, the ſeed being brought from that part of the River Nile where it falls into the ſecond lake. Here is alſo the beſt white grain, called mazza di Congo, that is, grain of Congo, and maize, which is of ſo little value that they give it to pigs, rice being likewiſe little thought of. Maize is known as mazza Manputo, that is, Portugal grain.

The variety of trees is ſo great as to produce sufficient fruit to ſupply nearly the whole population with food. Amongſt them are citrons, lemons, and, above all, luſcious orange-trees, whoſe fruit is neither ſweet nor acid, but is eaten without harm. The aforeſaid Duarte Lopez relates (to ſhow the fertility of the country), that he had ſeen a kernel of the citron left in the rind of that fruit, from which in four days a ſmall ſtem was ſpringing. There are other fruits called Bananas, which are ſuppoſed to be the Muſes of Egypt and Syria, but in thoſe countries they grow as large as trees, and are cut every year to increaſe their fruitfulneſs. They are delightfully fragrant, and very nutritious. Various ſpecies of palms grow likewiſe in theſe plains, one being the date palm, and another, the Indian nut, called Coccos, as within the latter is a head reſembling an ape; and they have a cuſtom in Spain, when wiſhing to frighten children, to mention the word Coccola. Another palm ſimilar to the above grows here, from which oil, wine, vinegar, fruits, and bread are all extracted. Oil is made from the pulp of the fruit, which is of the colour and ſubſtance of butter, but of a greeniſh hue; and this oil the people burn. It alſo ſerves as butter, and to anoint the body. They preſs the oil from theſe fruits in the ſame way as it is got from the olive, and then preſerve it by boiling. Bread is made from the kernel of the ſaid fruit, which is like an almond, but harder, and within it is the marrow, good for food, wholeſome and nutritious. This fruit, together with the pulp, is entirely green, and is eaten either in that ſtate or cooked. Wine is found in a hollow at the top of the tree, where it forms a ſort of trough, and from it is diſtilled a liquor reſembling milk, which for a few days is ſweet, then becomes acid, and in proceſs of time bitter, and is uſed with ſalad. When drunk freſh it acts medicinally, and, in conſequence, the people of thoſe countries do not ſuffer from gravel or ſtone. It cauſes intoxication to any who drink too freely of it, but otherwiſe is very nutritious. Other trees here produce a fruit called Cola, about the ſize of a pineapple, within which are other fruits, like cheſtnuts, containing four ſeparate pulps of red and carnation colour. Theſe are held in the mouth, and by maſtication and eating aſſuage thirſt, and taſte like water.

They preferve and ftrengthen the ftomach, and, above all, are valued in liver difeafe. It is faid that if the liver of a fowl or any fimilar bird is fprinkled with the juice of this fruit, it becomes quite frefh again even after decompofition. This fruit is in common ufe, and being fo abundant is very cheap. Other wild palms, alfo producing fruits for food, are here, whofe leaves are woven into mats, and made into coverings for houfes, and alfo into bafkets, and fimilar articles of everyday ufe. Trees called Ogheghe produce a pale yellow plum, of good flavour, and very fweet perfume. From thefe trees they cut off the branches, and plant them in fuch manner that they take root, and grow up very large, making ornamental paliffades round the houfes. On them they place woven mats, which, forming an enclofed court-yard, ferve as a fhade from the heat of the fun. In the midft of thefe enclofures are wooden houfes covered with thatch, not having ftories, but a ground floor, which is divided into convenient rooms, lined with mats of delicate make, and ornamented in various manners. And, here it muft be remarked, that thefe people do not build their houfes in this paftoral manner from lack of materials, for the mountains of Congo furnifh quarries of various valuable ftones, from which might be cut columns, architraves, bafes, and other large blocks, for building anything that was required. Indeed, it is faid fome maffes are of fuch enormous fize, that a whole church might be cut out of a fingle piece of the ftone like that which forms the obelifk, now ftanding before la Porta del Popolo. Befides thefe, there are the mountains producing porphyry, jafper, and white and coloured marbles, which in Rome are known as Numidian, African, and Ethiopian marbles, fome columns of which are in the Gregorian Chapel. Other marbles are found here, and amongft them very fine ones inlaid with jacinths, which are gems, and form veins on the mother ftones, and thefe, when feparated and arranged in fmall pieces, can be formed fo as to look like pomegranates. Columns, obelifks, and fuch-like works of art can be made from this marble, which fparkles as if ftudded with beautiful jewels. Befides thefe are other precious ftones, having an appearance of metal, of various colours, fome green and fparkling, others copper-coloured, and from which ftatues and other objects of great beauty might be made. There is, therefore, no lack of material, for the mountains abound in the above-mentioned ftones, and with others alfo, there being more here perhaps than in the whole world befide. Here are alfo lime, timber, animals for drawing and carrying, and every other requirement for building purpofes. But architects, mafons, carpenters, and all fuch workmen are wanting, and for the building of churches, walls, and other ftructures in thefe countries, men are brought from Portugal. Tamarind, caffia, and cedar-trees grow to fuch an extent on the banks of the River Congo, that fhips without number can be built from them, and thefe and other large and high trees are ufed alfo in houfe-building. The gardens produce every kind of vegetable and fruit, fuch as melons, water-melons, cucumbers, cauliflowers, and many others of like kind, which will not flourifh in our European climates.

CHAPTER II.

OF THE ORIGIN OF CHRISTIANITY IN CONGO; AND IN WHAT MANNER THE PORTUGUESE ACQUIRED THE TRADE OF THAT COUNTRY.

King Dom João II., wifhing to difcover the Eaft Indies, fent feveral fhips along the coaft of Africa, which, having found the Cape Verde Iſlands and the Iſland of St. Thomas, and running all along that coaſt, reached the River Zaire, already ſpoken of, where the natives proved friendly and civil, and did good trade with them. Later, he ſent other veſſels alſo to traffic with Congo, and, finding the merchandiſe open and profitable and the people amicable, ſeveral Portugueſe remained there to learn the language, and to trade, amongſt whom was a prieſt from Meſſa. The Portugueſe, meeting with the Lord of Sogno, uncle of the king, a courteous man, who at that time lived at the port of Praza, which is the mouth of the Zaire, were looked upon and reverenced by him almoſt like gods come down to live on the earth. But the Portugueſe told him they were men like himſelf, and Chriſtians, and ſeeing themſelves ſo much eſteemed by the people, the prieſt and the reſt began to reaſon with the Prince about the Chriſtian faith, and to ſhow the errors of paganiſm, and by little and little to teach him our religion, ſo that the prince, being much pleaſed with what the Portugueſe told him, became a convert. In this ſpirit of truſt and devotion, the Prince of Sogno went to Court to tell the king of the doctrines of the Chriſtian Portugueſe, and to encourage him to receive the Chriſtian faith. Then the king ſent for the prieſt to Court, that he might hear from himſelf what the prince had told him, and he, alſo, when he had heard, expreſſed his wiſh to become a Chriſtian. At this time thoſe veſſels returned to Portugal, by which the King of Congo ſent petitions to King Dom João II., of Portugal, begging for prieſts to be ſent him to propagate Chriſtianity, and the prieſt wrote at length alſo, by requeſt of the king, giving full information of all that had occurred. So the king ſent him prieſts, ornaments for the churches, croſſes, images, and everything elſe neceſſary for ſuch ſervice. Meantime the Prince of Sogno ceaſed not day and night to difcourfe with the Portuguefe prieft, having him in his houfe and at his table, to teach himfelf, and alfo the people, the Chriftian religion, favouring Chriftianity in every way in his power, fo that it might grow and take root in that country; the people and the king perfevering in the defire to be purged of all their abominable fuperftitions, and awaiting the Portuguefe veffels, with provifions for baptifm, and other neceffaries for this object. At laft, the fhips arrived with the expected means, which was in the year 1491 of our era, and anchored at the mouth of the Zaire. The Prince of Sogno, with demonftrations of great joy, met them with all his followers, and faluted and took them to his own houfe. The next day that prince, by advice of the prieft who had remained there, began to build a church of trunks and boughs of trees, which he, in perfon, with his fervants went to the wood to cut down, and covered with them a fite for a church, in which were reared three altars, in honour of the Moft Holy Trinity, and where he was baptized, with his infant fon, calling himfelf Emmanuel, the name of our Saviour, and his fon Antonio, after the patron faint of Lifbon.

Now, if any one afks by what names the people of thefe countries called themfelves before becoming Chriftians, it will certainly feem incredible to be told that neither men or women had proper names, fuch as are ufed by rational beings, but adopted thofe belonging to plants, ftones, birds, and beafts. The lords took the names of the feveral provinces over which they ruled. As for example, the above-named lord, and firft convert to Chriftianity in Congo, was called Mani Sogno, that is Lord of Sogno, although known by the name of Emmanuel after his baptifm; but now nearly all bear Chriftian names learnt from the Portuguefe.

After the Celebration of High Mafs, one of the priefts who

had come from Portugal afcended a pulpit, and gave a fhort fermon in Portuguefe on the chief points of the new religion and faith which they were receiving, which fermon the prieft, who had remained there and learnt their language, interpreted more fully to the nobles affembled in the church. The people, owing to their prince's converfion, were gathered together in fuch numbers, that, not being able to get into the church, the prince went outfide to them, and repeated what had been faid, befeeching them with much emotion to embrace with him the Chriftian faith.

After this all the Portuguefe went to the Court to baptize the King, who expreffed a fervent defire for that rite, and the Prince of Sogno ordered many of his own nobles to attend them with trumpets, and finging, and other honours; he alfo commanded the people to provide victuals along the roads for their ufe. So great was the multitude who ran to fee the Portuguefe Chriftians, that it feemed as if the whole country were covered with people, who loaded them with kindneffes, finging and making founds with cymbals and trumpets, and other inftruments of the country. And it is pleafant to add that for 150 miles between the fea-coaft and San Salvador the roads were all clean and fwept, and abundantly furnifhed with food and other provifions for the Portuguefe. It was the cuftom in thofe countries, when the King and his Nobles went out, to clean and prepare the roads, but on this occafion it was fpecially done, the Portuguefe being honoured as heroes for bringing the King the gift of faith, for the welfare of his foul, and to every one alike the light of God and eternal falvation. After being three days on the road they met the king's efcort, who prefented them with all manner of refrefhments, and paid them great honour, as did other nobles fent by the king to meet the Chriftians, the bearers of fo much bleffing.

Within three miles of the city, all the Court came to meet the Portugueſe with great pomp, and with muſic and ſinging, ſuch as is uſed in thoſe countries at ſolemn feſtivals; and ſo great was the crowd that not a tree or a raiſed place but was covered with people running together to ſee theſe ſtrangers who had brought this new and life-giving religion. The king awaited them at the gate of his palace, ſeated on a throne, above a raiſed platform, and received them publicly, as is the ancient cuſtom with the kings of thoſe countries when ambasſadors arrive, or when tribute is brought, or on any other royal occaſion.

Firſt, the ambaſſador explained his miſſion from the King of Portugal, uſing as interpreter the prieſt above-named, and who was the chief means of the converſion of theſe people. After this the king roſe from his ſeat, and ſhowed by words and countenance the great joy he felt at the arrival of the Chriſtians, and ſat down again in preſence of his people. Theſe laſt, immediately after the ſpeech of the king, with ſongs and muſic, and other ſigns of delight, alſo manifeſted their ſatiſfaction with the embaſſy, and as an act of ſubmiſſion, proſtrated themſelves three times on the ground, and lifted their feet, according to the cuſtom of thoſe countries, praiſing and approving what their king had done, and cordially accepting the Goſpel which had been ſent to them from God, by the hand of theſe ſtrangers. Afterwards he was ſhown all the gifts ſent by the King of Portugal, and the veſtments of the prieſts, ornaments for the altar, croſſes, pictures of the ſaints, and banners. He liſtened with great attention, as, by his own deſire, they were all deſcribed one by one. Then the king retired and gave lodging to the ambaſſadors in a palace ſet apart for them, and the reſt were lodged in various houſes of the nobles, with every proviſion for their comfort.

Next day the king ſent privately for all the Portugueſe, when they deviſed the manner in which the baptiſm of the king was to take place, and how to effect the converſion of theſe people to the Chriſtian faith. After much diſcourſe, it was decided firſt to build a church, in which to celebrate with great ſolemnity the rite of baptiſm and other ſervices, and meanwhile to inſtruct the king and the people of the court in the truths of the Chriſtian religion. The king ſent to make great preparations with all ſorts of material, in the form of wood, ſtone, lime, and bricks, which the workmen and builders aſked for, who had come from Portugal to do the work. But the devil, who never ceaſes to mar good works, ſowed diſcord, and plots and hindrances aroſe againſt this growth of the Chriſtian faith, which threatened, by planting the croſs and the religion of the Goſpel, to deſtroy the devil's power in this kingdom, for the Anzichi, and alſo the people of Anzicana, living on both ſides of the River Zaire, from the falls before ſpoken of, and on towards the lake belonging to the King of Congo, began at this time to rebel. Now, this great river, being reſtrained by theſe falls, is greatly ſwollen there, and expands into a large and deep channel, from whoſe wideſt part riſe large and ſmall iſlands, one of which contains about 30,000 ſouls. In theſe iſlands, and in the places adjoining the river, the people roſe and turned againſt the government of the king, killing the governors ſent by him; ſo that during this rebellion, the ſpread of Chriſtianity was interrupted. The king then ſent his eldeſt ſon, named Maniſundi, who was governor of that region, to quell the rebellion, but it being neceſſary for the king to go in perſon, as the tumult increaſed, he wiſhed at once to be baptized, and ſo the work of the ſtone church ceaſed, and one of wood was haſtily raiſed. Together with the Portugueſe, the king in perſon gave orders how it was to be built, and within it he received the rite of Holy Baptifm, taking the name of Dom João, and the queen the name of Leonora, after the King and Queen of Portugal, and that Church was dedicated to the Saviour. This rebellion arofe amongft the above-named people, and not with thofe who live in the Iflands of the Great Lake, as is recorded in the firft book of the Hiftory of India, recently written in Latin; for that lake is nearly 200 miles diftant from the borders of Congo, and nothing was known of it in thofe days (and very little at prefent) except from hearfay. Befides, in that hiftory, from lack of records, the revolting people are called Mundiqueti, whereas the Portuguefe rightly call them Anziqueti.

Following the example of the king, many great nobles were baptized at the fame time as himfelf, having firft embraced fome of the principles of the Chriftian faith. After this the king went in perfon to put down the rebels, againft whom the prince his fon, and Manibatta, were already fighting. On arrival of the king the enemy fubmitted, and the king returned in triumph to the City of Congo, accompanied by his fon, who foon alfo became a Chriftian, taking the name of Affonfo, after the Prince of Portugal; and with him many noblemen and cavaliers, and other fubjects of his province embraced Chriftianity. Now the enemy of the Chriftian faith ftill purfuing his wicked efforts to impede the fpread of Chriftianity, and feeing he had gained nothing towards it by the war, put it into the mind of the fecond fon of the king not to agree to the new religion which his father, mother, brother and many of the nobles had embraced. Thus he fowed tares in his heart, and in thofe of other nobles who favoured his views, and who were more inclined to the vices of the flefh than to any virtue, being oppofed to the Gofpel command, now begun to be preached, that a man fhall have but one wife; which law to thefe people, accuſtomed to take as many wives as they pleaſed, was more difficult to accept than any other.

Thus the two brothers were ſeparated, each maintaining his own cauſe. The eldeſt, Dom Affonſo, defended the Chriſtian faith with great zeal, ſweeping away all the idols from his province; but his brother, who was called Pango, being governor of that province, oppoſed him ſo far as to enliſt moſt of the nobles on his ſide, amongſt them being ſome who had already been baptized, and whoſe wives, ſeeing themſelves ſeparated from their lords on account of the Chriſtian laws, ſpoke evil of the new religion, and ſpread ſnares around Dom Affonſo, trying to get rid of him, and ſo to ſtop the Chriſtian faith being ſpread abroad. All theſe, together with Pango, gave the king to underſtand that Affonſo favoured the Chriſtian religion in order to uſurp his place, and by means of it would rebel ſo far as to baniſh him from the kingdom. The king liſtened to theſe ſtories, and deprived the prince of the province he governed. But Divine providence, preſerving him for a great purpoſe, upheld his cauſe by means of certain people, who begged the king not to be moved to anger till he had firſt examined the proofs of guilt againſt the prince. He was eſpecially perſuaded to this by the counſels of Maniſogno, whom we have already ſaid was the firſt to become a Chriſtian, and took the name of Emmanuel, and who happened to be at court at this time. By his ſkilful reaſoning (being alſo the oldeſt courtier and lord of that time, and much beloved by the king and people), he got the king to retract the ſentence againſt Dom Affonſo. The king having afterwards inquired into the actions of his ſon, and finding the charges againſt him were falſe and malicious, reſtored him to his governorſhip, commanding him, however, not to proceed with too much rigour againſt the pagans, whilſt exalting the Chriſtian religion. But he, full of love and of the Divine Spirit, ceaſed not to ſpread the Goſpel faith, and to put into practice the commandments of God.

Therefore, his enemies never ceaſed pouring into the ears of the king all manner of deceit, in order to deſtroy what this good prince had built up, eſpecially as Maniſogno was now away governing his own province. Thus it came to paſs that there being no one left to defend the Chriſtian laws, the king began to doubt the faith which he had before ſo warmly embraced, and ſent again to recall the prince to court, to render account of the revenues received from the province he governed, intending after that to depoſe him from his governorſhip. But the prince, enlightened by his good angel, and diſcovering the ambuſhes of the enemies of God, delayed his departure, and ſoon his father, already old and infirm, paſſed away. His mother, however, who always remained firm in the Catholic faith, and dearly loving her eldeſt ſon, kept the death of the king concealed for three days, and, aided by her faithful friends, gave it out that the king had ordered no one to be admitted to him. Then in a ſecret manner ſhe informed her ſon by runners (who, placed at convenient diſtances, like poſts, are always ready to carry the commands of the king throughout the kingdom) of the death of his father, and that ſhe would keep it ſecret till he arrived, begging him to come without delay, and with as great haſte as poſſible to the court. Therefore (by means of theſe ſame poſts, and being carried by ſlaves, according to the cuſtom of the country, day and night), in one day and two nights, he accompliſhed with marvellous ſpeed, the journey of 200 miles, and ſuddenly appeared in the city.

CHAPTER III.

DEATH OF KING DOM JOAO, FIRST CHRISTIAN KING—THE SUCCESSION OF HIS SON, DOM AFFONSO, AND THE WARS AGAINST HIS BROTHER—OF THE MIRACLES WHICH HAPPENED, AND THE CONVERSION OF THIS PEOPLE.

Now together with the death of the king, was announced the ſucceſſion to the throne of Dom Affonſo. He followed his father to the tomb, accompanied by all the nobles of his court, and the Portugueſe, who, with funeral pomp not before ſeen by this people, performed the Chriſtian offices, and offered prayers for the dead. But thoſe who had before been adverſe to the new king, not feeling ſafe at court, united themſelves to Pango, who lived in the province of his government, and who, whilſt his father was ſtill living, was at war with the Mozombi and other rebellious tribes. Hearing of the death of his father, and that his brother was already on the throne, Pango conferred with the enemy. He then collected a great force, and came armed againſt his brother, bringing with him the greater part of his ſubjects, to the number of nearly 200 thouſand men. King Dom Affonſo awaited him in the royal city with the few who were friendly to him, ſupported by the good old man, Prince of Sogno, who was with him by reaſon of the Holy Religion of Chriſt, and of the allegiance he owed. He having made a liſt of friends ready to defend the place, found the number did not exceed 10 thouſand men, amongſt whom were about 100 Chriſtians of the country, beſides a few Portugueſe who happened to be there. Theſe people were but little prepared for ſuch an encounter, and not being reſolute, proved doubtful and timid, on account of the great army Pango brought with him. But the king, confident and unſhaken in his faith, and of aid from Heaven, reaſſured his men, together with the old chief, who ceaſed not day and night from his work, or from giving words of encouragement to thoſe who feared the aſſaults of the enemy, aſſuring them that God would be their help. Therefore, whilſt theſe awaited the approach of their adverſaries, the latter ſpread themſelves around the city to beſiege it, with ſo great a noiſe of trumpets, and tumult, and cries, and terrific threatenings, that the few who were inſide the city, loſing heart, the Chriſtians with the reſt, came to the king ſaying, they had no ſtrength to reſiſt ſuch a powerful army, and that it ſeemed better to them to make peace, and abandon the new religion ſo lately embraced, in order not to fall into the hands of their cruel enemies. But the king, full of religious zeal, reproved them for their perfidy, calling them cowards, and faithleſs, but ſaid if they wiſhed to go over to the enemy they were to do ſo; notwithſtanding he would, with the few who followed him, truſt in God's help, knowing human aid was vain againſt such an immenſe army; and without aſking them to join hands with him, or to riſk their lives, he only begged them to remain and ſee what would happen. Yet they, being ſtill faint-hearted, determined to leave the king, and gathering together, went forward outſide the city, where they met the good old Prince of Sogno, who, with a few of his men, had come out to reconnoitre the enemy's camp, and to make neceſſary proviſion. To him they told what they had already ſaid to the king, declaring it was madneſs to imperil their lives with ſo few men againſt a great multitude, and that, without doubt, it was better to ſurrender, and ſo be ſafe. To which the old man replied, with Chriſtian courage, that they muſt not ſo ſuddenly loſe hope, but do as the king had told them and truſt in Jeſus Chriſt, the Saviour of the world, whoſe faith they had but lately received with ſo much zeal, and who would infallibly ſuccour them; nor would he have them, from fear of man, turn from the holy doctrine which they had embraced with ſo much fervour, reminding them that they would not have to fight with ſtrangers, nor with people of remote countries, but with their own relations and countrymen, ſo that they ſhould not loſe any opportunity of reconciliation and friendſhip.

He alſo ſaid to them, Behold, my age is now one hundred years, and yet I take arms, being zealous for the religion which I have adopted, and for the homage and honour I owe to my king, and do you, who are in the flower of your age, ſhow timidity and ſo little fealty to your lawful ſovereign? At leaſt, if you will not fight yourſelves, animate your vaſſals, and do not diſcourage them, but let us await the firſt encounter of the enemy, and we ſhall have time after that in which to make plans for our ſafety. With theſe comforting words he re-aſſured the fallen ſpirits of theſe men, and they turned back with him to ſeek the king, who was in the church praying, and aſking help from God. They waited until he came out, and then fell on their knees before him, entreating pardon for their weakneſs and cowardice in having wiſhed to abandon their prince in this hour of extreme peril, ſaying, alſo, that they reſolved conſtantly to defend him and the laws which they had received, and that they would fight for him even unto death. But the king, who ſaw that this aid came ſtraight from God, gave thanks ſilently in his heart, at the ſame time vowing to ſacrifice himſelf to maintain his faith. Then, with a ſmiling countenance, he turned and ſaid, I believe, O Lord, that Thy greatneſs is infinite, and that Thou canſt do all things, making much from little and little from much, when it pleaſeth Thee, and I doubt not that Thou canſt bring to aid my weaknefs Thine own invincible ftrength, fo that by Thy favour, even with thefe few weak ones, I may become conqueror, not only of this army, but alfo of far greater ones if need be. And I promife (O my God), in addition to what I have faid, to exalt Thy true faith, Thy holy name, and the doctrine of Thy falvation all the days of my life. In witnefs of which confeffion he at once caufed a crofs to be placed in the middle of the fquare oppofite the church. It was conftructed by the prieft, and meafured eighty hands high, with a crofs-beam of proportionate width. Now the Eternal God, recognizing the faith which had prompted this vow of the good king, was pleafed to comfort him with a heavenly vifion, in the form of a bright and beautiful light, at fight of which he fell on his knees in tears, lifting his eyes and hands to heaven, not being able to fpeak for weeping, but fhowing by figns that his fpirit was in a ftate of rapture from what he faw. All prefent did the fame, and loft their eyefight for the fpace of nearly an hour by reafon of the brightnefs of the light; then, by degrees, lifting their eyes to heaven, they faw five flaming fwords engraven thereon, which for the fpace of about an hour, remained fixed in a circle, but could never be underftood or defcribed by thofe who faw them. Which fwords the king took for arms, as is feen on the royal feal, ufed from that day to this, and even by the king who now lives and reigns. The crofs itfelf, placed there on account of a vow, and of the miracle which happened, may be feen ftill on the fame fite in front of the church, which derives its name from it, of Holy Crofs.

This crofs (the old one being much worn by time, and fallen down) the late king, Dom Alvares, father of the prefent one, reftored to its former condition, in memory of that miracle. The vifion greatly confirmed the minds of the citizens, who were before wavering, whilft it ftruck terror into thofe of the oppofing party, when they heard of it. Notwithftanding, Pango fent to tell the king, and all who were with him, that if they did not immediately furrender, give up the city, and make him king by oath, and alfo abandon the new religion, they muft all be flain, but if they complied with his demands they would be pardoned. To which the lords who were with the king fent anfwer that they were ready to die in defence of their prince, and for the Chriftian religion. The king efpecially fent word that he was not afraid of his threatenings, at the fame time that it grieved him to the heart, as his brother, to fee him walking in darknefs, and far from the way of light; adding that the kingdom belonged to him of right, not having ufurped it, and the law which he had received came of a certainty from God, who would defend and fuccour him. He befought him to put away his falfe faith taught by the devil, and to be baptized fo as to become a fon of God, and merit eternal falvation. Then the king fent for jewels, and rich robes from his houfe, and in order to encourage thofe lords who took part with him, gracioufly diftributed them amongft them all, thereby giving fo much fatiffaction that they refolved to follow the king's inftructions with renewed courage. The fame night almoft half the bafer people bearing arms rebelled, and fled to the camp of Pango, giving him to underftand that the king and all who were with him had loft heart, and already thought of faving themfelves, but that they could only do fo by taking the road to the river, which, as we have faid, was a mile in defcent from the city.

At the end of that road, between the river and the mountain, was a fmall marfh on the right, two feet deep; and on the left were the mountains, and the garrifon of Pango, who befieged the aforefaid mountain fo as to leave no other means of exit but by paffing over this marfh, which was the length of a gunſhot, and led directly to the river. Pango, believing what he had been told, ſent at once to ſtop up that paſſage with ſharp ſtakes driven firmly into the marſh, covering them with water, ſo that when the enemy fled in the darkneſs of night, they might ſuddenly be enſnared thereby and undone. The ſame night Pango and his army waited eagerly for the dawn, in order to aſſault the city, pondering how beſt to do ſo. But Dom Affonſo, confeſſing himſelf and communicating, together with his faithful allies, awaited the foe, who, ſecure of victory, had already made over to the chief men of his army the poſſeſſions of thoſe left in the city, and the various governments of the kingdom. In the early morning Pango led the aſſault with furious impetus on the ſide of the city that faces to the north, where the great plain, ſinking through a narrow gorge, becomes a baſin, almoſt circular, and ſurrounded by hills, with an exit diſtant a gunſhot from the ſite of the city, which is a level space two miles in circumference, on which lies, as we have before ſaid, the city, the church, the reſidences of the nobles, and the court of the king. Here Dom Affonſo, and his handful of men, were ranged againſt the pagans and his brother; but before the latter had come face to face with the king, he was ſuddenly and entirely routed, and put to flight. Seeing himſelf conquered, Pango was greatly amazed, not underſtanding the cauſe of his defeat. Notwithſtanding, he returned next day to the aſſault in the ſame place, and again was diſcomfited in like manner, but took refuge in flight, clearly recognizing that his defeat was not from the valour of his enemies, but the reſult of a miracle. Therefore, the people in the city mocked at the pagans, and taking heart from ſuch a victory, no longer feared, but became eager to attack their adverſaries, who told them that they had not won the day themſelves, but owed their victory to the presence of a lady in white, whose dazzling splendour blinded the enemy, whilst a knight riding on a white palfrey, and carrying a red cross on his breast, fought against and put them to flight. On hearing this, the king sent to tell his brother that these were the Virgin Mary, the mother of God, whose faith he had received, and St. James, who were sent from God to his aid, and if he would become a Christian he would have the like favour. Not in any way consenting to this, Pango spent the night in arranging for the conquest of the city from two positions, one being by the narrow pass we have already spoken of, with part of his army; the other by way of the river where no guards were, and which he attempted to pass with another division of his men, led by himself. The latter made the first onslaught and were routed, and Pango, hoping to push on to the other side whilst his enemies were defending the pass, fell into a trap, for those who were in the city, hearing that Pango was coming by that way, hastened thither to repulse him and his forces. They fought with such fury against him, that being overcome by fright, he rushed headlong into the ambush covered with stakes, which he had himself prepared for the Christians, and there, almost maddened with pain, the points of the stakes being covered with poison, and penetrating his flesh, he ended his life.

With this victory, and the death of his brother, the king was freed from farther opposition, and knowing that his followers were wandering about, and afraid of appearing before him on account of their misdeeds, he sent, like a good prince, to announce to them that he pardoned their former ill-conduct, and would receive them with favour. They all submitted, except the captain-general, named Manibunda, who, fearing to come before the king on account of his treachery, at length obtained pardon, and did deeds of penance by helping in the work of building the church. He afterwards became ſo devoted and humble a Chriſtian, that the king wiſhed to leſſen his puniſhment, but Manibunda reſolved to continue his labours until the edifice was finiſhed. Peace being eſtabliſhed in the kingdom, the king commanded the principal church, called Holy Croſs, to be finiſhed, which was ſo called as a remembrance of the croſs planted there, and becauſe the foundation ſtone was laid on the feaſt of Holy Croſs. He ordered, beſides, that the men ſhould carry the ſtones, and the women the ſand, which they fetched from the river. The firſt to carry ſtones on his ſhoulders and throw them into the foundation was the king, the queen doing the ſame with the ſand, as an example to the lords and ladies of the court, and to encourage the people in the holy work. Thus the building, being helped forward by all manner of workpeople, was quickly raiſed, and maſſes and divine ſervice celebrated with much ſolemnity. Many became Chriſtians, and ſo great a number of nobles and others aſked for baptiſm that there were not found prieſts ſufficient to perform the ſervice. After theſe events the king ſent the ambaſſador of the King of Portugal, who had been detained till now at the court by theſe diſturbances, and with him another ambaſſador of his, named Dom Rodrigo, and alſo ſome of his own and this ambaſſador's relations to Portugal, that they might learn the Chriſtian doctrine and alſo the language, and give an account to the king of the paſt events. Beſides this, he aſſembled the governors from the different provinces at a place arranged for them to meet in, and told them publicly, that whoever poſſeſſed idols or anything elſe contrary to the Chriſtian religion, muſt give them up to the deputies appointed to receive them, and that all who kept them back would be burnt, and receive no pardon. This threat being at once put into execution, in leſs than a month were brought to the court all the idols, ſorcery books, and magic writings, which had been worſhipped as gods. And truly great numbers of theſe things were collected, for each perſon worſhipped what moſt ſuited his taſte, apart from any ſenſe of rule or reaſon, ſo that there were numerous demons of ſtrange and frightful forms. Many held in great reverence winged dragons, which they nouriſhed in their private houſes, giving them the moſt coſtly viands to eat; others ſerpents of horrible ſhape, large goats, tigers, and various monſtrous animals; and the more they were ugly and deformed the more they held them in honour, regarding as ſacred, unclean birds, ſuch as bats, ſcreech-owls, and the like. In fine, they choſe for gods, ſerpents, beaſts, birds, plants, trees, various kinds of wood and ſtone, carving alſo on wood and ſtone, repreſentations of the above to form pictures. And not only did they worſhip living animals, but alſo thoſe ſtuffed with ſtraw.

The act of adoration was performed in various ways, but always in the direction of humility, ſometimes throwing themſelves on their knees and taking up mouthfuls of earth, covering the face with duſt, and making prayer to the idols both in words and geſtures, and offering ſacrifices of the beſt things they poſſeſſed. They had alſo their ſorcerers, who told theſe ſimple people that the idols ſpoke to them, and deceiving them ſo far that if any ſick preſented themſelves and were healed, the ſorcerers aſcribed the cure to the idols, but if they were not healed they ſaid the idols were angry. This was the ſort of religion practiſed amongſt the people of Congo before they received baptiſm and the knowledge of the living God. Now the king having collected together from the different houſes in the city all theſe falſe gods, commanded, that in the ſame place where, a ſhort time before, he had fought and conquered his brother's people, every one ſhould bring a piece of wood, till a great pile was raiſed, and there caſt in the idols and all other things which they had treated before as ſacred, ſo that all might be burnt. Then he aſſembled all theſe people together, and in place of their idols gave them croſſes and images of the ſaints, which he had received from the Portugueſe, and commanded each of his lords to build a church, and erect croſſes in the city of the province where they ruled, as he had given them example. After this he announced to them and to the people, that he had ſent ambaſſadors to Portugal, to bring back prieſts who would teach them religion and adminiſter the holy ſacraments, and ſhow the way of ſalvation; alſo to bring images of God, of the Virgin Mary, and of the ſaints, to diſtribute amongſt them, and that they muſt meanwhile remain ſteadfaſt in the faith. This was, however, ſo rooted in their hearts already that they no longer thought of the idols and falſe gods which they had given up. He ordered them alſo to build three churches, one of which was dedicated to the Saviour, in gratitude for the victory given, and in which the kings of Congo are buried; and from it the royal city takes the name, as has been ſaid, of San Salvador. The ſecond church, dedicated to the Virgin Mary, was called Our Lady of Help, in remembrance of the ſuccour given againſt their enemies. The third was dedicated to St. James, in honour and memory of the miracle effected by that ſaint, who fought on the ſide of the Chriſtians, appearing amongſt them on horſeback.

Meanwhile the Portugueſe ſhips arrived, bringing numerous teachers of the Holy Scriptures, with friars and prieſts of the Orders of St. Francis, St. Dominic, and St. Auguſtine. Theſe all, with much charity and zeal, diſſeminated the catholic faith, which was received alike by every one in the kingdom. The prieſts themſelves were treated with as great reverence as if they were ſaints, being worſhipped by the people on their knees, who kiſſed their hands and aſked for benediction every time they met them.

Theſe prieſts on arriving in the provinces inſtructed the people in the Chriſtian faith, and taking back with them ſome of the natives, taught them the heavenly doctrine, ſo that they might tell it to the people of their own tribes in their own tongue. In this manner, in proceſs of time, the Catholic faith took root in thoſe regions, and continues even till now, although it has ſuffered not a little damage, to which we ſhall allude later.

CHAPTER IV.

DEATH OF KING DOM AFFONSO, AND SUCCESSION OF DOM PEDRO—FIRST COLONIZATION OF THE ISLAND OF ST. THOMAS—OF THE BISHOP SENT THERE—OF THE DEATH OF TWO PRINCES THROUGH CONSPIRACIES OF PORTUGUESE, AND OF CONGO NOBLES—HOW THE ROYAL LINE BECAME EXTINCT—DISSENSIONS AMONG THE PORTUGUESE—AND VARIOUS GREAT EVENTS RELATING TO RELIGION.

WHILST theſe matters were progreſſing for the ſervice of God, and Chriſtianity alſo was ſpreading with rapid growth, it pleaſed God to call to Himſelf King Dom Affonſo, who, at his death, gave tokens of the ſincerity of his paſt life, for he died in great faith, declaring his hour was come, and ſpeaking of the Chriſtian religion with ſo much love and truſt, as left no doubt that the croſs and true faith of our Saviour Jeſus Chriſt were imprinted in his heart. Above all, he commended to Dom Pedro, his ſon and ſucceſſor, the Chriſtian doctrine, which he, following the example of his father, took care to defend and maintain. In this king's time a greater number of veſſels began to arrive in thoſe parts, and the Iſland of St. Thomas was occupied by the Portugueſe, by command of the King of Portugal, for before thoſe days it was all barren inland, and its ſhores only inhabited by a few ſailors, who came from the neighbouring countries. This iſland being in proceſs of time well populated by the Portugueſe and other people, who went there by permiſſion of the king, and having a large trade, for the land, as has been ſaid, was well cultivated, the king ſent a biſhop, to rule over the Chriſtians living in the iſland, and alſo over thoſe in Congo. Now, on his arrival in the Kingdom of Congo, it was wonderful to ſee the joy with which he was received by its king and people, as, all the way from the ſea to the city, a diſtance of 150 miles, the roads were prepared and ſwept, and covered everywhere with mats. The people were particularly ordered, at certain ſpaces ſeverally appointed to them, to prepare the roads in ſuch manner that the biſhop ſhould not ſet his foot upon any undecorated ground. But the moſt curious ſight was the immenſe multitude of people, men and women even climbing trees and other high places where they might ſee the biſhop, whom they looked upon as a holy man ſent from God. Some offered him ſheep and goats, others fowls, game, fiſh, and various kinds of food in ſuch quantities that the greater part had to be left behind. In this manner, theſe newly-made Chriſtians ſhowed their zeal and obedience.

Above all, one muſt remark that as the biſhop paſſed along, numbers of men, women, and children of all ages, as well as old men of eighty years and upwards, preſſed forward with every ſign of real faith, to aſk for the water of holy baptiſm. Nor would they allow the biſhop to paſs until he had given what they required; ſo that in order to ſatiſfy them he was greatly ſtayed on his way, and obliged to carry water with him in certain veſſels, as well as ſalt, and other proviſion neceſſary for the rite. Not to mention all the welcomes given to the biſhop wherever he went, or the lively joy univerſally, as well as peculiarly ſhown on his arrival at each place, we ſhall only ſay that the biſhop arrived at laſt at the City of San Salvador, having been met by the prieſts, the king, and the whole court, with whom he went in proceſſion to the church, and after giving thanks to God, was conducted to the houſe aſſigned him by the king. He commenced at once to ſet in order and reform the church itſelf, and to give good rules to the prieſts and friars who lived there. He alſo conſtituted the ſaid church to be the Cathedral Church of Holy Croſs, which had at that time attached to it about twenty-eight canons, various chaplains, a chapel maſter, and choriſters, beſides being provided with an organ, bells, and everything elſe neceſſary for Divine ſervice. But this biſhop labouring in the Vineyard of the Lord, now in Congo, and now in the Iſland of St. Thomas, going and coming by ſhip between the two in twenty days, and always leaving vicars in his abſence, at laſt died, and was buried in the Iſland of St. Thomas.

To him ſucceeded a negro biſhop in Congo, a deſcendant of the royal houſe, who had been ſent by King Dom Affonſo firſt to Portugal, and afterwards to Rome, where he learned Latin and the doctrines of Chriſtianity; and, having returned to Congo, after diſembarking, he ſet out for his biſhopric of San Salvador, but died on the way. Now many years having paſſed ſince a biſhop was appointed to this kingdom, and the above-named king being dead and leaving no ſon, he was ſucceeded by his brother, Dom Franciſco, who alſo only lived a ſhort time. The fifth in ſucceſſion, and alſo neareſt the royal line, was King Dom Diego, a man of noble mind, witty, intelligent, prudent in counſel, and, above all, an upholder of the Chriſtian faith. He was alſo a great warrior, ſo that in a few years he conquered many of the neighbouring countries. This king was greatly attached to the Portugueſe, adopting their dreſs, and giving up his native attire. He was magnificent both in his own clothing and the arrangements of his palace; he was alſo liberal and courteous, giving freely, both to his own people and the Portugueſe. He paid large ſums for anything that pleaſed him, aſſerting however that coſtly things ſhould only be worn by kings, and after wearing a dreſs two or three times he gave it to his followers. Whereupon, the Portugueſe, ſeeing this king valued cloths of gold, tapeſtries, and ſuchlike rich ſtuffs, they brought him them from Portugal; and from that time the people of this kingdom began to ſet great value on tapeſtries, cloths of gold and ſilk, and all ſuchlike lordly furniture.

In the reign of this king there was a third Bishop of St. Thomas and of Congo, a Portugueſe by birth, who was received with all the uſual ceremonies on the way, and at the Court of San Salvador. Now the enemy of the Chriſtian faith being greatly troubled at the happy progreſs of the Catholic religion, began to ſow diſſenſion amongſt the friars and prieſts, and their biſhop, which aroſe from the long liberty they had enjoyed without the ſuperviſion of a paſtor, for each one conſidered himſelf not only as good as the biſhop, but even a better man than he was, and would yield no obedience to their prelate, thus cauſing grievous ſcandal and wicked example amongſt them. But the king, like a true Catholic, always took part with the biſhop, and to make an end of theſe diſturbances ſent ſome of the prieſts priſoners to Portugal and others to the Iſland of

St. Thomas. Some alſo went away of their own accord, taking their poſſeſſions with them. So that inſtead of the Chriſtian doctrine growing, it rather diminiſhed, and this from the fault of thoſe who taught it. Nor did the adverſary ſtop here, for he alſo ſpread diſcord amongſt the ſubjects and their rulers, three princes ſtarting up, after the death of this king, to claim the ſucceſſion at the ſame time. The firſt was the king's own ſon, who was not favoured by many of the people, as they wiſhed for another; therefore he was killed at once. There remained two others of royal blood, one of whom was made king by his followers, with the conſent of the greater part of the people, and againſt the will of the Portugueſe and certain lords, who aimed at placing the other on the throne. Whereupon, the above-mentioned lords, together with the Portugueſe, went to the church to kill the newly-elected king, thinking that if they did ſo the other muſt of neceſſity reign. At the ſame time the oppoſite party killed the king choſen by the Portugueſe, perſuading themſelves that he alſo being dead there would be no difficulty in obtaining the kingdom for their king, becauſe there was none other left to whom the royal ſceptre belonged by law. So that, at the very ſame hour, but in different places, both theſe kings were murdered. In the midſt of theſe conſpiracies and ſlaughters, the people, ſeeing that there were no longer any legitimate ſucceſſors to the royal crown, and blaming the Portugueſe for all the evils which had happened, turned againſt and ſlew as many as they found there, not however touching the prieſts, either in that or in any other places where they lived.

There being therefore no one of royal blood upon whom to beſtow the government, a brother of the late King Dom Diego, Dom Henrique by name, was choſen. He, going to a certain war againſt the Anzichi, left as Governor, with the title of King Dom Alvares, a young man twenty-five years old, who was the ſon of his wife by a former huſband. This ſame Dom Henrique died ſhortly after the war was ended, and the above-named Dom Alvares was by common conſent choſen King of Congo, to whom all paid allegiance. With the death of Dom Henrique the royal line of the ancient kings of Congo became extinct.

But Dom Alvares being a juſt and wiſe and mild ruler, it was not long before the tumults of the kingdom were at an end. He gathered together all the Portugueſe who had been ſcattered throughout the neighbouring provinces during the paſt rebellions, as well the prieſts as the laity, and by this means did much to eſtabliſh the Catholic faith, for he vindicated them, and clearly ſhowed to all that the Portugueſe had not brought about the paſt troubles. Having alſo determined to write a full account of all that had happened to the King of Portugal, and alſo to the Biſhop of St. Thomas, he deſpatched certain people with theſe letters. The Biſhop, who had been afraid to go to the Kingdom of Congo during the height of the late rebellion, on receiving theſe tidings ſet out at once for that country, where he uſed his authority in appeaſing diſſenſions, giving inſtructions at the ſame time for Divine ſervice, and the office of the prieſts. Soon after this he returned to his Biſhopric of St. Thomas, and there being attacked with illneſs died, and thus for a third time theſe parts were left without a biſhop.

It came to paſs in conſequence of there being no biſhop, that the king, his nobles, and people began to grow ſomewhat cold in the Chriſtian faith, and to indulge greatly in the ſins of the fleſh. The king eſpecially was led to do this by ſome young men of his own age, with whom he was intimately aſſociated, and particularly by one of the nobles, who was a relation of his own, called Dom Francifco Bullamatare, that is to fay, catch ftone. This man, taking great liberties on account of being a great noble, and having for fome time kept aloof from Chriftian inftruction, gave out in public that it was a foolifh thing for men to have but one wife, and that it was better to return to their former cuftoms in this matter; and fo the devil by means of this man opened the door for the deftruction of the temple of Chriftianity in that kingdom, which till then had been eftablifhed at the coft of fo much labour. All thefe young men went fo far from the way of truth, that, going on from fin to fin, they almoft entirely gave up the true faith.

Meanwhile, the above named Dom Francifco died, and, being a great noble, was buried in the Church of Holy Crofs, although he had clearly not forfaken his falfe religion. But it came to pafs (marvellous to fay, and as a fign to confirm the righteous in their holy faith, but to terrify the wicked) that at night evil fpirits took off part of the roof from the Church of Holy Crofs, where this man was buried, and with horrible founds, heard throughout the whole city, dragged his body from the grave, and carried it away. In the morning the gates of the church were found fhut, but the roof was broken open, and the tomb of that man empty.

By this fign the king was firft warned of the grave error he had committed, as well as his affociates. Neverthelefs, there being no bifhop in that kingdom, and although the king remained firm in the Chriftian faith, yet being ftill young, and unmarried, he continued to indulge in the fins of the flefh, until punifhed by God with other fevere difcipline.

CHAPTER V.

INCURSIONS OF PEOPLE CALLED JAGGAS INTO THE KINGDOM OF CONGO — THEIR CUSTOMS AND WEAPONS — THE SEIZURE OF THE ROYAL CITY.

For there came unexpectedly to devaſtate the Kingdom of Congo certain people living like Arabs, and ancient Nomads, who are called Jaggas, and have their dwellings near the firſt lake of the River Nile, in a province of the Empire of Monemugi. They are a cruel and murderous race, of great ſtature and horrible countenance, and eat human fleſh, but are very courageous and valiant in battle. Their weapons are pavices, darts, and daggers. In their cuſtoms and everyday life they are very ſavage and wild, and go entirely naked. Theſe people have no king, and live in huts in the foreſt, after the manner of ſhepherds. They went wandering up and down, putting to fire and ſword, and ſpoiling and robbing every part of the country through which they paſſed, till they reached Congo, which they entered through the province of Batta. Overthrowing thoſe who were firſt to reſiſt them, they then went on to the City of Congo, where the king was, and who had loſt heart from the victory gained by his enemies in Batta. Neverthelefs, he went out with ſuch ſoldiers as he had againſt theſe adverſaries, and in the very ſame plain where Pango in former years fought with King Dom Affonſo, this king joined battle with his foes. In this encounter, the king being partly diſcomfited, retired into the city, where not feeling ſafe, but forſaken of God on account of his ſins, for he lacked the ſame truſt in Him which King Dom Affonſo had, he reſolved to leave the city a prey to his enemies. He then fled to a certain iſland on the River Zaire, called Horſe Iſland, accompanied by the Portugueſe prieſts and the principal nobles of the kingdom. The Jaggas being thus left in poſſeſſion of the royal city, and indeed of the whole kingdom, the inhabitants fled for ſafety to the mountains and deſert places, whilſt the enemy ſet fire to the city and the church, deſtroying all before them, and ſlaying without mercy all who came in their way; ſo that after dividing themſelves into ſeveral armies, they got the maſtery, now in this province and now in that, all over the country.

In this perſecution every one in the kingdom ſuffered, the king, the people, the Portugueſe, and their prieſts, each according to his degree; ſo that the poor people wandering about the country died from lack of food and all other neceſſaries. The king alſo and his followers who had taken refuge in the above-named iſland, it being a ſmall one, and the people many, all ſuffered ſo terribly from lack of proviſions, that the greater part died of famine and peſtilence. The price of a ſmall quantity of food roſe to that paid for a ſlave, who was ſold for at leaſt ten crowns.

Thus, forced by neceſſity, the father ſold his ſon, and the brother his brother, every one reſorting to the moſt horrible crimes in order to obtain food.

Thoſe who were ſold to ſatiſfy the hunger of others were bought by Portugueſe merchants, who came from the Iſland of St. Thomas with proviſions, the ſellers ſaying that they were ſlaves, and in order to eſcape farther miſery, theſe laſt confirmed the ſtory. In this manner great numbers of ſlaves, natives of Congo, are found in the Iſland of St. Thomas, and in Portugal, who were ſold during that time of diſtreſs, and amongſt them ſome of royal blood, and others chief nobles. Therefore the king clearly knew that it was on account

o

of his miſdeeds ſo much miſery had come upon them, and although as king he had not to ſuffer hunger, yet he did not eſcape the terrible malady of dropſy, his legs ſwelling enormously, and this diſeaſe was cauſed by the bad air and food, and dampneſs of the iſland, which infirmity remained with him till his death. Grieved to the heart by theſe calamities, the king was converted to God, aſking pardon for his offences, and doing penance for his ſins. He ſent ambaſſadors, by advice of the Portugueſe, to aſk for help from the King of Portugal, to whom they were to relate all theſe recent miſſortunes. This happened in the beginning of the reign of King Dom Sebaſtian, who with much kindneſs immediately ſent ſuccour by a captain, called Franciſco de Gova, who had fought in divers wars in India and Africa. He took with him 600 ſoldiers, and beſides them a great number of gentlemen adventurers who joined the expedition.

CHAPTER VI.

THE KING OF PORTUGAL SENDS HELP AND AN AMBASSADOR TO THE KING OF CONGO—THE LATTER REFUSES TO ALLOW THE MINES OF CONGO TO BE DISCOVERED BY THE KING OF PORTUGAL—THE KING OF CONGO SENDS AMBASSADORS TO SPAIN TO ASK FOR PRIESTS, AND TO CARRY SPECIMENS OF METALS FROM THE MINES—THE EVENTS WHICH BEFELL THEM—THE VOW OF DUARTE LOPEZ.

THE captain bore commands from the king, that the Iſland of St. Thomas ſhould provide him with ſhips, victuals, and all things neceſſary for this enterpriſe. On arriving with theſe proviſions at Horſe Iſland, where the king ſtill was, the Portugueſe took him away with them, and gathering together all the armed people in the country, they marched againſt the enemy as quickly as poſſible, and after fighting with them from time to time in the field, at the end of a year and a half the king was reſtored to his throne; yet they conquered by the noiſe and power of the guns, rather than by numbers, the Jaggas being greatly terrified by thoſe fire-arms.

Thus, in spite of their reſiſtance theſe foes were driven out of the Kingdom of Congo, and but few returned to their homes. The Portugueſe captain, after remaining a quarter of a year to ſee the king reſtored to his poſſeſſions, returned to Portugal, bearing letters from the King of Congo, to aſk for prieſts in order to eſtabliſh the Chriſtian religion, but ſeveral Portugueſe who had accompanied the captain to theſe parts remained behind, where they are to this day, having gained great wealth and poſſeſſions. Being again at the head of his kingdom, and peace reſtored, the king became a good Chriſtian and married Donna Caterina, who ſtill lives; and by her had four daughters, and by one of his own ſlaves two ſons and a daughter. Females not succeeding to the throne in thoſe countries, the eldeſt ſon inherited it, alſo called Dom Alvares, who reigns to this day. Whilſt the aforeſaid captain was in Congo, King Dom Sebaſtian hearing that there were mines of gold, ſilver, and other metals in that country, ſent two ſkilled workmen, who had been employed by the Caſtilians for the ſame purpoſe in the Weſt, to ſearch for theſe mines, and make ſome profit out of them.

But a Portugueſe, called Franciſco Barbuto, the intimate friend and confeſſor of the King of Congo, perſuaded him not to allow theſe mines to be diſcovered, aſſuring him that if this happened, by degrees he would loſe his independence in the kingdom. For this reaſon the king directed the artificers to be led by ways where he knew they would find no mines.

And as the king forbade the working of metals in the Kingdom of Congo, and ſuch things were greatly prized in Europe, any farther large trade ceaſed to be carried on with thoſe countries, the Portugueſe merchants not caring to venture there, and conſequently but few prieſts either. For theſe reaſons, and others of which we have already ſpoken, the Chriſtian religion became very lukewarm in Congo, till at laſt it almoſt died out. But King Dom Alvares, as has been ſaid, after ſo many troubles ſent him by God in puniſhment for his miſdeeds regarding religion, ſaw his error, and became a good Chriſtian. He was alſo very friendly to the Portugueſe, calling them his ſons, and doing whatſoever they wiſhed. Above all, he never relaxed his endeavours to ſecure prieſts and others learned in the Scriptures, ſending ambaſſadors again to Portugal, to aſk for ſuch aid as would ſecure the maintenance of the Catholic faith, which from lack of prieſts to teach the people and to adminiſter the ſacraments, was almoſt forgotten in the kingdom. And this, moreover, not from any fault on the part of the people, they being marvellouſly well inclined towards the holy faith.

The above-named captain having arrived in Portugal, and preſented theſe requeſts to his king, had no other anſwer than words, the king, who was ſtill a young man, promiſing to do what he aſked, but taking no farther trouble to ſend prieſts or teachers to Congo.

Therefore the king of Congo ſent another ambaſſador, a relation of his own, Dom Sebaſtian Alvares by name, together with a Portugueſe, to aſk for prieſts, and alſo to gather together the natives of Congo, who we have ſaid had been ſold as ſlaves from ſheer neceſſity, and taken to the Iſland of St. Thomas, and to Portugal. Some of theſe remained, however, of their own free will in ſlavery, but a great number were ranſomed and brought home to their own country, by whoſe means, and eſpecially by the help of many lords and nobles found amongſt them, the king was enabled to re-eſtabliſh the Chriſtian religion, which had ſuffered great loſs, and alſo to employ them as valuable counſellors and miniſters of ſtate in his kingdom, their long captivity having given them much experience of the world. The King of Portugal graciouſly promiſed the above-named ambaſſador that prieſts ſhould be ſent to Congo, yet he alſo returned there without any. Three years after this King Dom Sebaſtian ſent a biſhop, called Dom Antonio de Gilova, chiefly for the Iſland of St. Thomas, but alſo gave him a commiſſion to viſit the Kingdom of Congo. On his arrival at St. Thomas's Iſland he found the governor oppoſed to him, and ſo ſailed to Congo. Here alſo he was perſecuted by the ſaid governor and his friends in Congo, who gave the king to underſtand that the biſhop was a man of ambitious and haughty ſpirit, and very obſtinate, and therefore ill-affected towards himſelf and his Court. The king at firſt was induced by theſe accuſations to forbid the biſhop entering his kingdom; nevertheleſs, afterwards he received him with great honour, ſending one of his ſons to meet and accompany him to the city. There he remained nearly eight months, and then went away, leaving two friars and four prieſts behind him; and this was before the King of Portugal went to Africa. This king having been overthrown in Africa, and the biſhop gone, the King of Congo wrote to Dom Henrique, the Cardinal, now raiſed to the throne of Portugal, to beg that prieſts might at once be ſent him, but he obtained nothing at his hands, as the Cardinal only lived a ſhort time.

To Dom Henrique ſucceeded Don Felipe, King of Caſtile, who ſent to announce his acceſſion to the throne, to the Governor of St. Thomas's Iſland, giving him letters alſo for the King of Congo to the ſame purpoſe. Thereupon the governor despatched Sebastian de Costa, with title of ambassador, to convey the royal letters to the King of Congo. Having delivered the letters, and concluded all necessary affairs of state, the King of Congo sent him to the Court of King Don Felipe, with a reply to his letters, at the same time offering to show him the mines of metal, to which the Portuguese kings, his ancestors, had been denied access, and also sent various specimens of those metals. He particularly added a request, that the king would at once send him a sufficient number of priests, and gave a full account of the miserable condition to which his people were reduced as regarded the Christian religion, by reason of the past disturbances in the country. This Ambassador, Costa, died on the way, his vessel being wrecked on the coast of Portugal, which sad news was learnt (all the men being drowned) from letters found in a chest, cast on the shore by the waves, and which also contained the particulars of his embassage to the king.

Having heard what befell Costa, the King of Congo, never relaxing in his pious endeavours to preserve the Christian religion in his kingdom, determined to send another ambassador to Spain; and after various obstacles, several lords of his court competing for the honour, the king at last, in order not to give offence to any of them, chose Duarte Lopez, a Portuguese, from whose lips Pigafetta took this present history, and put it in writing.

This Lopez having lived for some time in those parts, was well experienced in the ways of the people, and happening to be at court just then, was employed at once by good favour of the king, who gave him full instructions in writing, with regard to his mission to his Catholic Majesty in Spain, and to His Holiness the Pope, at Rome. He also furnished him with letters of credit and authority to both, and passports, and all things eſſential to his poſition, eſpecially recommending him to all other Chriſtian princes, and begging them to beſtow on him the conſideration befitting an ambaſſador.

The ſum of his embaſſage was, that he ſhould convey letters to King Don Felipe, and relate to him fully the condition to which the Kingdom of Congo had been reduced in conſequence of the late wars, and from lack of prieſts, and that he ſhould aſk his Majeſty to ſend a ſufficient number of confeſſors and friars to eſtabliſh the Goſpel in thoſe remote regions, where the people had ſo lately been converted to Chriſtianity. Beſides this, he was to preſent him with various ſpecimens of metals, and other things, and proffer to him in the name of the King of Congo a free traffic in the ſame, although this right had been denied to his anceſtors.

Duarte was alſo, on behalf of the King of Congo, to kiſs the Pope's feet, and deliver his credentials. At the ſame time he was to recount the great miſery and loſs his people had gone through for the ſake of the Chriſtian religion, and to commend theſe ſouls to His Holineſs, praying him, as Supreme Head of all Chriſtians, to have compaſſion on ſo many of the faithful, who, from lack of prieſts to teach the Chriſtian faith, and adminiſter the Bleſſed Sacraments of the Church, were gradually going to perdition.

Having received his deſpatches, Duarte quitted the court, and ſpent nearly eight months in tranſacting various matters for the king in thoſe parts; but at laſt, in January, being then ſummer in Congo, he embarked in a certain veſſel of 100 tons burden, which was bound with its cargo for Liſbon. Now ſailing along, he reached the ocean where the Cape Verde Iſlands lie, and there the veſſel, which was an old one, ſprang a leak in the prow. Therefore, as a ſtrong wind was blowing in front, and they were unable to reach the abovenamed iſlands, or the mainland of Africa, much leſs to continue their voyage, ſailing with the ſhip cloſe to the wind, and ſtraining a veſſel which already leaked ſo much, the pilot thought it better to turn his courſe, and taking the wind in the poop, run for ſhelter to the Iſlands of New Spain. In fine, after terrible diſaſters, and great danger of being loſt, or periſhing for lack of proviſions, with much toil they reached the Iſland of Cubagoa, which lies over againſt the Iſland of St. Margherita, where they fiſh for pearls. From thence, after haſtily repairing the ſhip, and taking in proviſions, they ſailed by a ſhort route to the mainland, going into harbour at Cumano, or as it is called, the New Kingdom of Granada in the Weſt Indies. This battered veſſel having reached a place of ſafety, ſunk at once to the bottom, the paſſengers however being ſaved, though ſcarcely alive after the hardſhips they had endured from hunger and thirſt, and above all, from the horrible ſtorms of that tempeſtuous ocean.

Whilſt the aforeſaid ambaſſador was trying to regain his health, the fleet of ſhips ſailed, which went every year from thoſe ſhores to Caſtile, ſo that he was obliged to wait for the next fleet, and ſpend a year there, beſides having nothing to do. In the meantime the King of Congo, having received no tidings of his Duarte, nor heard of his being driven by ſtreſs of weather into the Weſt Indies, but regarding him as dead, was ſtill ſteadfaſt in his purpoſe to reſtore Chriſtianity in his kingdom. Therefore he ſent another ambaſſador, called Dom Pedro Antonio, who was ſecond perſon in the realm, with the ſame demands. He was accompanied by Gaſparo Diaz, the chief Portugueſe, and richeſt and oldeſt inhabitant in the kingdom; ſo that no means were left untried whereby the King of Spain might be induced to grant theſe requeſts. The ambaſſadors had ſpecial commands if they found Duarte Lopez, to confer with him in their negotiations.

But this expedition had a ſad end, for their ſhip was captured by Engliſhmen, whilſt being towed towards the Engliſh coaſt, and afterwards wrecked. Dom Pedro Antonio and his ſon were drowned, but a few were ſaved, and amongſt them Gaſparo Diaz, who arrived in Spain when Lopez had already entered on his embaſſy at court. Now this Gaſparo wrote to tell Duarte he wiſhed to return to Congo without going to court, whether on account of the death of the cardinal king, or for ſome other reaſon, one cannot ſay, but ſo he did.

During the time our Duarte was in the Weſt Indies, where the climate is in all reſpects the ſame as that of Congo, he noticed the people of thoſe parts differed in the colour of their ſkin from thoſe in Congo. For in Congo the people are uſually black, but in the Weſt Indies almoſt white, that is to ſay, between white and black, and are called Mulattos by the Spaniards. This clearly ſhows the colour of the ſkin is not owing to the heat of the ſun, but to ſome natural cauſe, which to this day has never, either by ancient or modern writers, been fully underſtood.

His health being reſtored, Duarte ſailed to the port of the City of San Domenico, in the Iſland of Hiſpaniola, that he might take paſſage by the firſt ſhip to Caſtile. He happened to find a Portugueſe veſſel amongſt thoſe ready to join the fleet going to Caſtile, as in that way it went in greater ſafety.

The wind being favourable, all theſe ſhips arrived in company at Terceira, one of the iſlands called Azores, which means Sparrow Hawks, and from thence ſailed to San Lucar de Barrameda, the harbour at the entrance of the River Guadalquiver, and ſo on to Seville. Duarte Lopez then ſet out for Portugal to ſee his own family, and to provide himſelf with all things neceſſary, finally arriving at Madrid, where

P

the court at that time happened to be. Here he was courteoufly received by his Catholic Majefty, to whom he declared the object of his embaffy. But now many difficulties arofe, and various accidents croffed and hindered the courfe of affairs which he had to accomplifh in the name of the King of Congo. For foon after his arrival the fad news reached him of the death of the King of Congo, by whom he was fent, and added to that, King Dom Felipe was occupied in the conqueft of England, fo that his negotiations were not forwarded, but only delayed from time to time, nor did he fee any means of defpatching them; and, indeed, he was given to underftand that at that time he would gain no attention.

Now this fame Duarte, overcome by fo much adverfity, and calling to mind his paft perils and grievous fufferings, endured during a long and terrible voyage, and feeing that at one time he was making progrefs, but at another going back in his negotiations, felt alfo that in this world there is no comfort except in God Almighty. He was continually oppreffed with grief at the thought of being unable to relieve the people of Congo in their prefent extremity, knowing affuredly in what danger they were of going to eternal perdition, and the heavy burden of daily expenfes incurred by himfelf and his family at court was another fource of diftrefs. In fine, he had no hope of ever bringing to effect the matters which had been entrufted to him by the King of Congo, and fo made choice of another courfe, which was as profitable in itfelf as it was healthful to his foul. For the Good Angel having touched his heart, with manly courage, he abandoned the fword, and took up the crofs, renouncing the world and its deceitful pomps. Habited in a grey coarfe drefs, he left Madrid, and went to Rome, in order to lay before Pope Sixtus V. the matters of his embaffage, for he would not neglect the wifhes of that king who had fent him, although he had aſcended to a better life. He was graciouſly received by His Holineſs, to whom he related the miſerable condition of the people of Congo, touching the worſhip and ſervice of God, from lack of prieſts to teach them the Chriſtian doctrine, and to adminiſter the ſacraments of the Church; for an innumerable multitude of people preſented themſelves every day for baptiſm, inſtruction, confeſſion, and communicating. Moreover, Lopez, in addition to the vow he had made, determined to uſe the wealth with which God had bleſſed him in Congo (and that was by no means ſmall) for building a houſe, wherein for the ſervice of God certain learned men, and ſundry prieſts ſhould reſide, to inſtruct the youth of thoſe countries in different languages, in liberal arts, in the doctrine of the Goſpel, and the myſteries of our ſalvation. From which houſe, as it were, out of a holy ſchool, there might come forth learned men from time to time, well inſtructed in the divine laws, who ſhould be able in their own tongue to arouſe anew, and ſpread abroad the Chriſtian faith, now almoſt aſleep and dried up in thoſe regions, thereby proving fruits of bleſſing, and ſouls vigilant for the Chriſtian faith. Hereto he meant to add a hoſpital, which ſhould be a ſhelter for God's poor, who, arriving from foreign countries, would be received into that hoſpice to be healed of their infirmities.

With this purpoſe, therefore, he went to Rome, and to obtain licenſe from His Holineſs to build this ſeminary and hoſpital, at the ſame time beſeeching him to grant jubilees, indulgences, and other diſpenſations requiſite for ſuch good and Chriſtian works, in thoſe countries ſo far remote from Chriſtendom.

Having preſented himſelf to the Pope, and delivered his letters of credit, he then fully recounted the tenor of his miſſion, and had a gracious hearing. But the Pope gave him to underſtand that the Kingdom of Congo belonging to the King of Spain, he would refer the matter to him.

CHAPTER VII.

OF THE COURT OF THE KING OF CONGO—OF THE DRESS OF THE PEOPLE OF CONGO BEFORE, AND AFTER THEY BECAME CHRISTIANS—OF THE ROYAL TABLE AND THE MANNERS OF THE COURT.

HITHERTO we have clearly ſeen how the Chriſtian religion took riſe in Congo, and the ſucceſſive ſtrange diſaſters which befell it. Now it is time to deſcribe alſo the manners and cuſtoms of the court of this kingdom. In ancient times the king and his courtiers, as we ſaid before, wore garments made from the palm-tree, which hung from the girdle downwards, and were faſtened with belts of the ſame material, of beautiful workmanſhip. In front alſo, they wore as an ornament, and made like an apron, delicate ſkins of civet cats, martens, and ſables, and alſo by way of diſplay, a cape on the ſhoulders. Next the bare ſkin was a circular garment, ſomewhat like a rochet, reaching to the knees, and made like a net, from the threads of fine palm-tree cloths, taſſels hanging from the meſhes. Theſe rochets which were called Incutto, they threw back on the right ſhoulder, ſo as to leave the hand free, and on the ſame ſhoulder carried a zebra's tail, faſtened to a handle, according to an ancient cuſtom in thoſe parts. They wore very ſmall yellow and red caps, ſquare at the top, which ſcarcely covered the head, and were uſed more for ſhow than as a protection from the ſun or atmoſphere. For the moſt part the people went barefoot, but the king and ſome of his nobles wore ſandals, after the antique, like thoſe ſeen in Roman ſtatues, and theſe were alſo made from the palm-tree. The poorer ſort and common people wore the ſame kind of garments, from the middle downwards, but of a coarſer cloth, the reſt of the body being naked. The women wear three kinds of aprons; one long, reaching from the waiſt to the feet, the ſecond ſhorter, and a third ſhorter ſtill, each apron having a fringe round it. Another garment is like a doublet, and reaches to the waiſt. They have alſo capes for the ſhoulders, all theſe coverings being made of cloth from the palm-tree. The women leave the face uncovered when out of doors, and wear the ſame kind of caps as the men. The common people dreſs in like faſhion, but in much coarſer materials. Slaves, and the loweſt of the people only wear garments from the waiſt downwards, the reſt of the body being entirely naked.

But ſince this kingdom received the Chriſtian faith, the nobles of the court have begun to dreſs according to the Portugueſe faſhion, wearing cloaks, capes, ſcarlet tabards, and ſilk robes, every one according to his means. They alſo wear hoods and capes, velvet and leather ſlippers, buſkins, and rapiers at their ſides. Thoſe not rich enough to imitate the Portugueſe, retain their former dreſs.

The women alſo have adopted the Portugueſe faſhions, wearing veils over the head, and above them black velvet caps, ornamented with jewels, and chains of gold round their necks; but this only refers to the ladies of the court, as the poorer women keep their former dreſs. After the king's converſion to Chriſtianity, his court was to ſome extent regulated like that of the King of Portugal, and ſpecially ſo for his ſervice at table. When the king eats in public, a throne with three ſteps is ſet up, covered with Indian carpets, and thereon are placed a table and chair of crimſon velvet, the latter being ſtudded with boſſes of gold. He always eats alone, no one ever ſitting at table with him, and the princes ſtand around with heads covered. His veſſels of ſervice are gold and ſilver, both for eating and drinking.

He maintains a guard of the Anzichi and other tribes, who ſtand around his palace, armed with the weapons already mentioned; and, when he goes abroad, the drums are beat, which can be heard five or ſix miles off, ſo making it known the king has left his palace. All his lords accompany him, and alſo the Portugueſe, in whom he puts great truſt, but he ſeldom quits his palace. Only twice a week he gives audience in public, and then he ſpeaks to none but the great men. No one poſſeſſing eſtates or lands, but all belonging to the Crown, they have no diſputes, beyond a few words, nor have they any writing in the Congo tongue. Criminal caſes are treated lightly, being very ſeldom puniſhed with death, and the crimes committed by the Mociconghi (for ſo the people of Congo are called in their own tongue) againſt the Portugueſe, are judged by Portugueſe law. When any great wrong happens between them, the king baniſhes the offender to ſome deſert iſland, eſteeming it a greater puniſhment to exile a man from his fellows to the end he may do penance for his ſins, than to execute him at once. And if it happens that any thus baniſhed live for ten or twelve years, the king uſually pardons them if they are worthy of it, and even employs them in the ſervice of the ſtate as men who have been well schooled and humbled by ſuffering. In civil diſagreements it is arranged that if a Portugueſe has any diſpute with a Mocicongo it muſt be referred to a Congo judge, but if a Mocicongo ſues a Portugueſe, the matter is brought before the Portugueſe conſul and judge, for the king has granted this poſt to one of their own nation in that country. No writing is uſed in transactions, either between theſe people themſelves, or with the Portugueſe, nor have they any legal inſtruments, but all matters are tranſacted by word and witneſs. They preſerve no hiſtory of their ancient kings, nor any memorial of paſt ages, not knowing how to write. They uſually meaſure the ſeaſons by the moons, being ignorant of the hours of day and night, and are accuſtomed to ſay, in the time of ſuch an one, ſuch a thing happened. They do not reckon diſtances by miles or ſuchlike meaſurements, but by the number of days men travel, laden or unladen, from one place to another. Touching their marriage or other feaſts, they celebrate them by ſinging love ballads, and playing on lutes of curious faſhion. Theſe lutes in the hollow and upper part reſemble thoſe uſed by ourſelves, but the flat ſide, which we make of wood, they cover with ſkin, as thin as a bladder. The ſtrings are made of very ſtrong and bright hairs, drawn from the elephant's tail, and alſo from palm-tree threads, which go from the bottom to the top of the handle, each being tied to a ſeparate peg, either ſhorter or longer, and fixed along the neck of the inſtrument. From theſe pegs hang very thin iron and ſilver plates, fitted to ſuit the ſize of the inſtrument, which make various ſounds, according as the ſtrings are ſtruck, and are capable of very loud tones. The players touch the ſtrings of the lute in good time, and very cleverly with the fingers, having no key like the harp, but I do not know if I ſhould call the ſounds they call forth a melody, but merely ſuch as pleaſes their ſenſes. More than this (and very wonderful), by means of this inſtrument they indicate all that other people would expreſs by words of what is paſſing in their minds, and by merely touching the ſtrings ſignify their thoughts. They alſo dance and clap their hands together in time with the muſic. Pipes and flutes are alſo played with great ſkill at the king's court, whilſt the people dance ſomewhat in Mooriſh faſhion, with gravity and dignity. The common people uſe little rattles and pipes, and ſimilar inſtruments, which are harſher and ruder in ſound than thoſe uſed by the nobles.

In this kingdom ſimple medicines are made from herbs, trees, oils, waters, and ſtones, which Mother Nature has ſhown the people how to uſe. Fever is the moſt common malady, and prevails more in winter than ſummer, the rains bringing both heat and moiſture. Beſides, there is alſo what we call the French diſeaſe, known in the Congo tongue as Chitangas, but this is not ſo dangerous or difficult to cure in thoſe regions as with us. Fever they cure with a powder of red and grey ſandal-wood, which is the lignum Aquila. This powder is mixed with palm oil, and after anointing the ſick perſon two or three times with it, from head to foot, he recovers. For head maladies they apply certain small horns to the temples, firſt piercing the ſkin a little, and then ſucking the blood into the horn till it is full, uſing the ſame means for drawing blood from any other part of the body, when in pain, as a cure. This manner of blood-letting was practiſed alſo in Egypt.

The diſeaſe mentioned above as Chitangas, they cure with the ſame ſandal-wood ointment, the red being called Tavilla, and the grey Chicongo. The grey is moſt valuable, even a ſlave being given for a ſmall quantity of it. Purgatives they make from bark of trees, ground to powder, and taken in ſome kind of potion. Wounds are cured with the juice of herbs, and by applying the herbs themſelves, and Lopez relates having ſeen a ſlave who was pierced with ſeven mortal wounds from arrows, entirely reſtored by the juice of certain well-known herbs in that country.

So that theſe people are not encumbered with many

phyſicians for ſurgery, drugs, ſyrups, electuaries, plaiſters, and ſuchlike medicines, but ſimply heal and cure themſelves with ſuch natural plants as grow in their own country. Nor even of theſe have they great need, for, living as they do, under a temperate climate, and not gorging themſelves with a variety of food to pleaſe their appetites, nor taking much wine, they do not ſuffer from diſeaſes which are commonly the reſult of indigeſtion from over eating and drinking.

CHAPTER VIII.

OF THE COUNTRIES BEYOND THE KINGDOM OF CONGO TOWARDS THE CAPE OF GOOD HOPE, AND OF THE RIVER NILE.

HAVING deſcribed the Kingdom of Congo, the features of its ſituation, the people who inhabit it, and the neighbouring tribes, it remains for us to ſpeak briefly of the remaining portion of the coaſt-line of Africa, towards the Cape of Good Hope, which is the route to India as far as the Red Sea. Afterwards, when deſcribing the interior of the country, we ſhall refer to the River Nile, and to Preſter John and his kingdoms, in order, as far as poſſible, to give ſome knowledge of regions hitherto but little known. Beyond the Kingdom of Congo we may remember, is the country of the King of Angola, and farther towards the Cape of Good Hope that of King Matama, and the provinces ruled over by him, called Climbebe. This kingdom, as we have ſaid, extends from the firſt lake and the confines of Angola to the River Bravaghul, which riſes in the Mountains of the Moon, and unites with the River Magnice, which alſo ſprings from the firſt lake. The above-named mountains are divided from the Tropic of Capricorn towards the Antarctic pole, and beyond this Tropic lie the country and boundaries of the Cape of Good Hope, which are not governed by a ſingle king, but by ſeveral princes. In the interior, between this Cape and the Tropic, are the Mountains of the Moon, ſo greatly celebrated by the ancients, who believed the ſources of the Nile were to be found in them, which, however, is an error, as the poſition of the land indicates, and of which we have already ſpoken. This country has ſeveral high, rugged, and uninhabitable mountains, where the people are few, living like Arabs, in the open country, in ſmall huts, and clad in the ſkins of animals, being a wild and rude people, with but little honeſty, and permitting no ſtrangers near them. They uſe bows and arrows, and their food is fruits of the earth and fleſh of their cattle. Among theſe Mountains of the Moon lies a lake called Gale, whoſe weſtern ſide is ſmall, and from it flows the River Camiſſa, called by the Portugueſe Sweet River, which falls into the ſea at the Cape of Good Hope, near the point called Falſe Cape. Inaſmuch as veſſels coming from India firſt ſight a large cape called Agulhas, and afterwards a ſmaller one, the latter is called Falſe Cape, it being hidden from view by the real and great one. Between theſe two promontories the diſtance is 100 miles, showing the ſize of this famous cape, which, divided into two points like a horn, forms a gulf, and here Portugueſe ſailors frequently take in water from the river they named Sweet. The people on the coaſt living between theſe two points are black, although the Antarctic pole here reaches 35 degrees, and the people living high up in the coldeſt of the Mountains of the Moon are alſo black, a curious fact, and one for the information of thoſe who inveſtigate the effects of nature, and for philoſophers who ſpeculate whether the black colour is produced by the ſun, or by ſome other hidden cauſe, which I now leave undetermined. As this Cape is the largeſt, and extends farther into the ſea than any other in the world, and is difficult of paſſage, (as are all promontories) the ocean here alſo being fearfully tempeſtuous by reaſon of winds which blow off ſhore, cauſing many Portugueſe ſhips of extraordinary ſize to founder; moreover, not being known even by report to ancient Hiſtoriographers, and ſome time having elapſed ſince its diſcovery by the fleets of the King of Portugal, this ſeems a ſuitable place in which to give its dimenſions, and alſo ſuch information as may ſerve to ſhow how great was the paſſage between Portugal and India; the coaſt-line round the Cape of Good Hope alone extending nearly 6000 miles, of which we ſhall treat preſently.

Seeing that from the river of Fernando Poo, whence the above-mentioned cape begins to ſtretch into the ſea as far as the point called Cape Agulhas, it has a coaſt-line of more than 2200 miles from north to ſouth, and from the other ſide of the ſame point, as far as Cape Guardafuy, oppoſite the Iſland of Socotra, it reaches for more than 3300 miles from ſouth to north, the diſtance from Liſbon, along the coaſts of Africa and the Cape of Good Hope, as far as the Kingdom of Goa, is more than 15 thouſand miles. From thence to Malacca and China, and even farther, a long paſſage remains, ſo that at no time was greater or more perilous navigation undertaken, both with large and ſmall veſſels, than by the Portugueſe.

The Cape of Good Hope is ſo called, becauſe all who make its paſſage, both going and returning, chiefly conſider how they ſhall round it; and that being accompliſhed, the danger is conſidered paſt, and on account of this longing it is called the Cape of Good Hope.

Now to return to our ſubject, and to ſpeak of the Coaſt of Africa. Beyond Cape Agulhas there are alſo many ſafe ports and harbours, chief of which is the Bay of Formoſo. Next it is the Bay of the Lake, where the ſea forms a gulf, in which are iſlands and harbours. Beyond this the River St. Chriſtopher flows into the ſea, and at its mouth riſe three ſmall iſlands. From thence the coaſt-line ſkirts along a country called by the Portugueſe the Land of the Nativity, becauſe on that feſtival the land was firſt diſcovered, as far as Cape Peſchiera. Between this cape and the River Magnice lies the Kingdom of Buttua, which extends from the baſe of the Mountains of the Moon northwards to the River Magnice, and the country of Monomotopa; towards the weſt from the River Bavagul, and towards the ſea along the banks of the River Magnice. In this kingdom are ſeveral gold-mines, and the people reſemble thoſe of Monomotapa, as we ſhall hereafter ſhow. And ſo paſſing along the ſea-coaſt we find the River Magnice, on the frontier of the Kingdom of Sofala and of the Empire of Monomotapa.

CHAPTER IX.

OF THE KINGDOM OF SOFALA.

THE entrance to this kingdom is at the River Magnice, which flows from the firſt lake, out of which alſo the Nile riſes, and falls into the ſea between Cape Peſchiera and that called Cape Corrientes, ſituated 23 degrees and a half ſouth, under the Tropic of Capricorn. Three celebrated rivers run into it near the ſea, and the principal one, St. Chriſtopher, was ſo called by the Portugueſe, from having been diſcovered on that ſaint's day, although known to the natives as Nagoa. The ſecond took the name of Lourenzo Marques, who firſt diſcovered it. Theſe two rivers riſe in the Mountains of the Moon, which were held in great repute by the ancients, and called by the people of the country Toroa. In theſe mountains the ſources of the famous River Nile were ſuppoſed to be, but it was an error, inaſmuch as the firſt lake is not formed by waters from theſe mountains, being indeed very far off, and a low plain lying between it and them. The waters iſſuing from them, flow towards the eaſt, and increaſe the ſize of other large rivers, ſo making it impoſſible for theſe waters to be diſtributed either as far as the lake ſpoken of above, or to the Nile. Above all, the Magnice, iſſuing from the firſt lake, takes a different courſe from that of the Nile, as it goes towards the eaſt, and unites with the two above-mentioned rivers. The third river, Atroe, takes its riſe on that ſide of the mountains, in which are the gold-mines of Monomotapa, and in ſome parts of this river gold-duſt is found in the ſand. Theſe three rivers enter the great Magnice near the ſea, and all four together unite in one ſtream, which flows into the ſea, forming a very wide eſtuary. From the mouths of this river, the Kingdom of Sofala extends along the ſea-coaſt, as far as the River Cuama, which takes its name from a caſtle and fortreſs ſo called, belonging to Mohammedans, and heathen. This river is known to the Portugueſe as the mouths of the Cuama, for at the ſea it divides itſelf into ſeven mouths, out of which riſe five iſlands. Many others lie higher up the river, and are all well populated by heathen. This river flows from the ſame lake and ſources as the Nile. Thus the Kingdom of Sofala lies between the two rivers, Magnice and Cuama, on the ſea-coaſt. It is ſmall in ſize, and has but few villages and towns, the chief place being an Iſland, lying in the river, alſo called Sofala, and which gives its name to all that country. It is peopled by Mohammedans, and the king himſelf belongs to the ſame ſect. He pays allegiance to the crown of Portugal, in order not to be ſubject to the government of Monomotapa. On this account the

Portugueſe have a fortreſs at the mouth of the River Cuama, trading with thoſe countries in gold, amber, and ivory, all found on that coaſt, as well as in ſlaves, and giving in exchange ſilk ſtuffs and taffetas, which they bring from Cambaia, where they are worn. The Mohammedans now living in thoſe regions are not natives of the country, but before the Portugueſe came into thoſe parts carried on traffic there, going in ſmall veſſels from the coaſt of Arabia Felix. When the Portugueſe became rulers of the country, the Mohammedans whom they found there remained, and at this day are neither heathen nor of the ſect of Mohammed. From the ſhores lying between theſe two rivers, Magnice and Cuama, ſtretches out inland the Kingdom of Monomotapa, which abounds in gold-mines, the metal being carried into all the neighbouring provinces, to Sofala, and to other parts of Africa. It is ſaid, that from theſe regions the gold was brought by ſea which ſerved for Solomon's Temple at Jeruſalem, a fact by no means improbable, for in theſe countries of Monomotapa are found ſeveral ancient buildings of ſtone, brick, and wood, and of ſuch wonderful workmanſhip, and architecture, as is nowhere ſeen in the ſurrounding provinces.

The Kingdom of Monomotapa is extenſive, and has a large population of Pagan heathens, who are black, of middle ſtature, ſwift of foot, and in battle fight with great bravery, their weapons being bows and arrows, and light darts. There are numerous kings tributary to Monomotapa, who conſtantly rebel and wage war againſt it. The Emperor maintains large armies, which in the provinces are divided into legions, after the manner of the Romans, for, being a great ruler, he muſt be at conſtant warfare in order to maintain his dominion. Amongſt his warriors, thoſe moſt renowned for bravery, are the female legions, greatly valued by the Emperor, being the ſinews of his military ſtrength. Theſe female warriors, whoſe weapons are bows and arrows, burn the left breaſt with fire, in order to prevent it being a hindrance in ſhooting, as was the cuſtom of thoſe Amazons of olden time, ſo greatly lauded by the writers of early profane hiſtory. They are extremely agile and rapid in their movements, and above all ſhow great daring and courage whilſt fighting. In battle they reſort to very warlike manœuvres, retiring at times as if put to rout, and taking flight, yet turning round to aſſail their adverſaries with arrows; and, on ſeeing the enemy, elated with victory, already beginning to diſperſe, they ſuddenly turn and repulſe them with great ſlaughter. So that on account of their wiles and cunning, as well as rapidity of action in battle, they are held in great dread in thoſe regions. The king grants them certain lands, where they live alone, but at various periods they mix with men choſen by themſelves; and any male children born amongſt them are ſent to theſe men's houſes, but the females are kept apart by themſelves, and brought up in the arts of war.

This Kingdom of Monomotapa lies as it were on an iſland formed by the ſea-coaſt, by the River Magnice, by a portion of the lake from which the latter flows, and by the River Cuama. Towards the ſouth it borders on the territory of the Rulers of the Cape of Good Hope, before mentioned, and on the north is bounded by the Kingdom of Monemugi, as we ſhall ſhow preſently.

Now returning to our ſubject, which is a ſurvey of the ſea-coaſt, we find, after croſſing the River Cuama, the ſmall kingdom of Angoche, on the ſea, ſo called from ſome iſlands of that name, ſituated right oppoſite to it, and inhabited by the ſame people, both Mohammedans and heathen, as are in Sofala; merchants who traffic in ſmall boats along this coaſt with the ſame kind of goods as do thoſe of Sofala.

A little beyond we come ſuddenly upon the Kingdom of Mozambique, ſituated 14 degrees and a half ſouth, which takes its name from three iſlands lying at the mouth of the River Meginchate, where is a ſafe and large port, capable of accommodating ſhips of every ſize. The kingdom is ſmall, but abounds in every kind of food, and is touched at by all the veſſels coming from Portugal and India to that country. In one of theſe iſlands, called Mozambique, which is the principal, and gives name to all the reſt, as alſo to the whole kingdom, and to the above-mentioned port, ſtands a fortreſs garriſoned by the Portugueſe, from which are proviſioned, and on which depend all the other fortreſſes on the coaſt. The fleets which ſail from Portugal to India if delayed in their paſſage, winter at Mozambique; and thoſe which come to Europe, from India, neceſſarily touch at Mozambique for proviſions. This iſland, when the Portugueſe diſcovered India, was the firſt from which they drew any knowledge of the Indian language; and where they found the pilots, who directed their courſe. The people of this kingdom are heathen, black, naked, and very rough, but excel in archery, and are excellent fiſhermen. Following the coaſt-line, we come upon another Iſland called Quiloa, not of great ſize, but ſingularly excellent in poſition, for the climate is temperate; it has trees always green, and produces every kind of food. It lies at the mouth of the River Coavo, which, iſſuing from the ſame lake as the Nile, flows for ſeventy miles towards the ſea, where it becomes a wide ſtream, and at its mouth forms a large iſland, peopled by Mohammedans and heathen. Weſtwards, towards the coaſt, lies the ſaid Iſland of Quiloa. The latter is peopled by Mohammedans, who are almoſt white, and well clad in ſilk and cotton garments. Their women wear ornaments of gold and jewels on the arms and neck, and have large quantities of ſilver veſſels; they are leſs dark than the men, and their forms finely proportioned. The houſes are well built of ſtone, lime, and woodwork, and the architecture alſo is good. The gardens and orchards produce various herbs and fruits. From this Iſland the kingdom takes its name, which extends along the coaſt from Cape Delgado, ſituated nine degrees ſouth, and as far as the above-named River Coavo.

In former times the Kingdom of Quiloa was chief of all the ſurrounding provinces, as well as of thoſe near the ſea; and, when the Portugueſe arrived in the country, the King was not only confident of being able to defend himſelf againſt them, but alſo of driving them from the places which they had already taken. Yet, the contrary happened, for on giving battle, the king was completely routed and put to flight, by the Portugueſe, who took poſſeſſion of the iſland, and obtained thereby great ſpoils and wealth. They built there a fortreſs, which, however, was afterwards deſtroyed by command of the King of Portugal, who conſidered it unneceſſary, there being others already along the coaſt.

But we muſt not leave unnoticed the Iſland of S. Lorenzo, ſo called from having been diſcovered by the Portugueſe on the feaſt of that martyr. It is nearly 1000 miles long, and lies right oppoſite the coaſt of which we have written, commencing on the right of the mouths of the Magnice, 26 degrees ſouth, and extending north till it terminates at the mouths of the River Coava, in the Kingdom of Quiloa. This iſland forms a channel between itſelf and the mainland, which at its entrance on the weſt is 340 miles wide, becoming narrower in the middle towards the Iſland of Mozambique, where the width is 170 miles, and the remaining part expands to a conſiderable extent towards India, ſeveral iſlands riſing out of it.

Ships going between Spain and India almoſt always, when not prevented by ſtreſs of weather, paſs through this channel. Truly this Iſland is worthy of a better population, for it has many good and ſafe harbours, and is watered by numerous rivers, ſo that the land produces every ſort of food. Rice, and other grain; vegetables, oranges, lemons, and various fruits, every kind of fleſh and fowl, wild boar, ſtags, and ſimilar animals, are all found here, ſo great is the fertility of the iſland. The fiſh alſo is excellent. The inhabitants are heathens, with a few Mohammedans, of olive-coloured complexion, that is, between brown and white. They are much given to war, their weapons being bows and arrows, and darts of light wood, tipped with iron, in the form of hooks. These laſt they throw with great dexterity. They uſe ſwords alſo, and have leather cuiraſſes, made from ſkins of animals, which protect them from the blows of the enemy. This Iſland is divided into various chiefdoms, enemies to one another, and all at perpetual warfare. Mines of gold, ſilver, copper, iron, and other metals are found here; but theſe barbarous people do not go beyond the Iſland, only coaſting along its ſhores in canoes, made from the trunk of a ſingle tree, and, for the moſt part, permit no ſtranger to come near to trade, or to have any dealings with them. Notwithſtanding, the Portugueſe trade at ſome of their ports without diſembarking, taking back Amber, wax, ſilver, copper, rice, and other things. In this channel lie ſeveral large and ſmall Iſlands, peopled by Mohammedans. The principal one is the Iſland of St. Chriſtopher, then that of San Spirito, and another, called Magliaglie; the reſt are thoſe of Comoro, Anzoame, Maiotto, and ſome others. But, again returning to the ſea-coaſt, and paſſing along from Quiloa, of which we have ſpoken, we find the Kingdom of Mombaza, ſituated 3 degrees and a half ſouth, which takes its name from an iſland peopled by Mohammedans, and alſo called

Mombaza, where a fine City ſtands, whoſe houſes for the moſt part are high, and furniſhed with ſculptures and pictures. The King, who is a Mohammedan, having reſiſted the Portugueſe, it happened to him as to the King of Quiloa, for this City alſo fell a prey to them, and they found in it gold, ſilver, and pearls in abundance, besides cotton cloths, gold and ſilver ſtuffs, and other valuables.

This kingdom, which lies between the confines of Quiloa and Melinda, is inhabited by Heathen and Mohammedans, and is ſubject to the government of Monemugi. Still farther it ſtretches into the Kingdom of Melinde, which, equally ſmall, extends along the ſea-coaſt to the River Chimanchi, in latitude two degrees and a half; and on the other ſide of that river reaches 100 miles into the interior as far as Lake Calice. Near the ſea, and along the banks of this river, is an extenſive country, peopled by heathen and light-coloured Mohammedans, whoſe houſes are built after our own faſhion. The ſheep are peculiarly large, being double the ſize of thoſe in our country, therefore they divide them into five quarters, counting the tail as one, which weighs 25 or 30 pounds.

The women are fair, and adorn themſelves in Moorish faſhion, with great diſplay, wearing ſilk robes, and on their neck, arms, and feet, chains of gold and ſilver. Out of doors they are covered with a thin ſilk veil, so that unleſs they wiſh it, they are not recognized. In this territory ſhips find good harbours and anchorage. As a rule, the people are friendly, truthful, and familiar with ſtrangers, and have at all times received and made much of the Portugueſe, confiding in them, and never doing them harm in any way. Near theſe two capes of Mombaza and Melinde, three Iſlands riſe out of the ſea, one called Monſia, another Zanzibar, and the third Pemba, all peopled only by white-complexioned Mohammedans. Theſe iſlands are very fruitful, like thoſe of which we have already ſpoken, the people being little given to warfare, and more ready to cultivate the land, eſpecially as ſugar is grown here, which they take for ſale in ſmall veſſels to the mainland, together with other products of that country.

Beyond the three above-mentioned Kingdoms of Quiloa, Melinda, and Mombaza, and inland weſtwards lies the large Kingdom of Monemugi, which is bounded on the ſouth by Mozambique and the Kingdom of Monomotapa, as far as the River Coavo, on the weſt by the River Nile, between the two lakes, and on the north by the Kingdom of Preſter John. Near the ſea-coaſt this Emperor is friendly with the kings of Quiloa, Melinde, and Mombaza, by reaſon of the trade carried on, and to inſure traffic with the coaſt, from whence great quantities of cotton cloth, ſilks, and other merchandiſe, arriving from various parts, are conveyed into theſe countries, being greatly valued there. Theſe people particularly prize the ſmall red glaſs beads, made in the Kingdom of Cambay, which they hang round their necks in ſtrings like necklaces, and uſe alſo as money, gold not being valued. Silk robes, which they wear below the waiſt, they alſo greatly prize; gold, ſilver, copper, and ivory being given in exchange for all theſe things.

But, on the other ſide, towards Monomotapa, ſuch ſanguinary wars are waged continually, that it is difficult to know who has the victory; for within this boundary are two rival powers, the greateſt and moſt warlike in all theſe regions. Thoſe going out to battle on the part of Monomotapa are the Amazons of whom we have ſpoken, and on that of Monemugi, the Jagas, ſo called by the Mociconghi, although known in their own tongue as Agagi, and who we have ſaid in former times greatly haraſſed the

Kingdom of Congo, being not lefs courageous and warlike than the Amazons. They are black, and of formidable appearance, and mark the upper part of the lip and cheeks with lines burnt in with hot iron. They alfo have a cuftom of turning their eyelids infide out, the fkin of which, being black, the whites of the eyes give a terrifying and diabolical expreffion to the countenance. They are large in ftature, but ill-proportioned, and live like wild beafts, and feed on human flefh. When fighting they fhow great courage, and ufe frightful noifes to terrify their enemies. Their weapons are darts, and they defend themfelves with leather fhields, which cover the entire perfon. Sometimes they encamp behind thefe fhields, when ftuck into the ground, to form a palifade; and, on advancing to fight, take refuge under them, whilft haraffing the foe by throwing darts. Thus by warlike ftratagems they torment the enemy, inducing him to bring out his arrows to no purpofe againft their targets, and, when they fee them all fpent, the Agagi renew the fight with redoubled vigour, putting to flight and killing their adverfaries. And thefe are the artifices they ufe towards their enemies and towards the Amazons.

But thefe laft, as we have faid, are well difciplined in military ftratagems, and overcome by their fwiftnefs and fkill in battle, being well affured if taken by their foes, they would be devoured. Therefore they fight with redoubled vigour fo as to conquer, and by all means efcape from fuch a favage and cruel multitude; neverthelefs, the warfare caufes great flaughter on both fides. Thefe Agagi live at the fource of the River Nile, where it flows northwards from the lake, and are found alfo within certain limits along both fides of the river, as well as on the weftern banks of the Nile as far as the fecond lake, and the boundaries of the Kingdom of Prefter John. Touching thefe Agagi, it was confidered convenient to add in this part of the hiftory what before was omitted. Between the confines of the Monemugi and of Prefter John dwell many inferior rulers, and light-coloured people, who are fubject fometimes to one, and fometimes to the other of thefe two princedoms, and are people of far greater ftature than the reft of the inhabitants of thofe countries.

CHAPTER X.

OF THE REST OF THE SEA-COAST AS FAR AS THE RED SEA —OF THE KINGDOM OF PRESTER JOHN, AND ITS BOUNDARIES—OF THE FAMOUS RIVER NILE, AND ITS SOURCE.

Now refuming our defcription of the coaft, next to the Kingdom of Melinde, and towards Cape Guarda Fuy there are feveral places with good harbours along the fhores, inhabited by Mohammedans of white complexion, and where fhips from various countries trade in the above-mentioned merchandife. The firft of thefe places is called Patee; the fecond, Brava; the third, Magadoxo; and the fourth, Affion. Still farther is the famous promontory of Guarda Fuy, which, on account of its fize and jutting out fo far into the fea, is well known to failors coming from India, Ormuz, and Arabia Felix. It is the place where the Portuguefe ufually wait and watch every year with their fleet for the Mohammedan veffels, which fail laden with valuable merchandife in thofe parts without licence, the Portuguefe themfelves being mafters of the trade and wares, both in fpices and every other merchandife they bring from India;

ſo that every year the Portugueſe fleet makes great ſpoils of theſe merchant veſſels, in the ſame way as do the Engliſh and French at Cape St. Vincent.

Now on rounding the ſaid Cape of Guarda Fuy, there are many other territories and ports of the Mohammedans, in the direction of the Red Sea, the firſt of which is called Meth, and the next, Barbora, where the white ſkin is no longer ſeen, but the people are all black. Then follow Ceila, Dalaca, Malaca, and Carachin.

This coaſt, in the language of the country, called Baragiam, is inhabited by a black race, who are valiant in arms, and wear cotton cloths from the waiſt downwards. The better ſort wear over their ſhoulders a cloak with a hood, called Bernuſſo, which is indeed the Roman Sagum. This region abounds in gold, ivory, metals, and every kind of food. Next follow the two mouths or entrances to what is well-known as the Red Gulf, or Sea, and which are formed by an iſland called Babelmandel. That towards the weſt is fifteen miles wide, and of ſufficient depth for all large veſſels to anchor in. The other is ſmall, being only five miles wide, and full of ſhallows and ſand-banks, ſo that the entire entrance extends a diſtance of thirty miles. The cape on the African ſide of the gulf is called Roſbel, and the other, towards Arabia Felix, Ara. From thence the weſtern coaſt of ſaid gulf extends as far as Suez, which is its fartheſt point northward, and 1200 miles from the entrance. All this gulf, on both ſides, near the banks, is thickly ſtudded with ſmall iſlands, and has very little depth of water, ſo that only in the middle of it navigation is ſafe, for the current ſetting in from the ocean with great ſwiftneſs, keeps the middle of the channel clear and deep, throwing the ſand back on the ſhores.

As we muſt now ſpeak of the Empire of Preſter John,

who is the greateſt and richeſt prince in all Africa, we ſhall briefly ſay that his territory at this time extends from the mouths of the Red Sea to the Iſland of Syene, which is under the Tropic of Cancer, excepting the ſhores of the ſaid ſea, which, through ſupineneſs, he has loſt for fifty years paſt, the Turk having deſpoiled him of them. So that the boundary of his dominion towards the north-eaſt and eaſt is the greater part of the Red Sea; on the north, Egypt and the deſerts of Nubia; and on the ſouth, the country of Moenemugi. In round numbers the empire of this Chriſtian king has a circumference of about 4000 miles. The principal City, and where he chiefly reſides and holds his Court, is called Belmalechi, and forms the ſeat of empire of many provinces, which are themſelves ruled by kings. The territory is rich, and abounds in gold, ſilver, precious ſtones, and every kind of metal. The people vary in complexion, being white, black, and tawny, and are of good height and pleaſant countenance. The courtiers and nobles are ſplendidly attired in ſilk robes, gold, and jewels; and there is a law for dreſs, according to the different degrees of rank, ſome being allowed to wear nothing but dreſſed ſkins. Theſe people are to ſome extent Chriſtians, inaſmuch as they obſerve certain ceremonies of the Hebrew law. On the feaſt of Our Lady, in Auguſt, all the Kings and principal nobles aſſemble in the above city to celebrate it, every one bringing the tribute he owes to the Emperor. The people alſo come on pilgrimage from all parts to join in this celebration.

A ſolemn proceſſion is formed, and from the church whence it iſſues is carried a life-ſize image of the Virgin Mary, made entirely of gold; the eyes of the ſaid image being formed of two large and magnificent rubies, and the whole of the reſt of the figure adorned and covered with jewels and various ornaments. This image is carried on a ſtage of gold, of wonderful workmanſhip.

In this proceſſion Preſter John, ſimilarly adorned with jewels, and like precious and rare things, and dreſſed in cloth of gold, appears in public either in a golden chariot or on an elephant. So great is the multitude who run to ſee this Image, that many die of ſuffocation in the crowd. This king is called by a corrupted word Preſter John, for the complete name is Bel Gian. Bel ſignifies ſupreme, perfect, and moſt excellent; and Gian means Prince, or Lord, and appertains to any one having territory or juriſdiction. Bel Gian therefore ſignifies Chief Prince, and thus conjoined pertains only to the King, who alſo bears the cognomen of David, in the ſame manner as the Emperors took that of Cæſar.

It remains for us now to ſpeak of the Nile, which does not riſe in the country of Bel Gian, nor in the Mountains of the Moon, nor, as Ptolemy writes, from two lakes lying eaſt and weſt of each other, with about 450 miles between them. For in the ſame latitude in which the above author places theſe two lakes, lie alſo the Kingdoms of Congo and of Angola, on the weſt; and the Empire of Monomotapa, and the Kingdom of Sofala, on the eaſt, the diſtance from ſea to ſea being 1200 miles. Now in this region Lopez aſſerted there is but one lake, which lies on the borders of Angola and Monomotapa, and is 195 miles in diameter. Of this lake the people of Angola give information reſpecting its weſtern ſide, and thoſe of Sofala and Monomotapa of its eaſtern. So that whilſt we have a full account of this one, and they make no mention of any other lakes, we may conclude there are no others in that latitude.

It is true that there are two lakes, but ſituated in quite a contrary direction to that of which Ptolemy writes; for he, as has been ſaid, places his evidently from weſt to eaſt, and thoſe we now ſee lie almoſt in a direct line north and ſouth, and nearly 400 miles apart. Some in thoſe countries think that the Nile iſſuing from the firſt lake flows underground and then reappears. Others deny this, but Lopez aſſerts as a reliable fact that the Nile does not flow underground, but running through deſert and lonely valleys without inhabitants, and having no ſettled channel, is therefore ſaid to flow underground.

The Nile certainly flows from the firſt lake, which lies in latitude 12 degrees ſouth, and is like a ſhell, and ſurrounded by very lofty mountains, the largeſt of which, called Cafates, are on the eaſt, and on both ſides are mountains producing ſaltpetre and ſilver. The Nile flows thence 400 miles due north, and enters another very large lake, which the natives call a ſea. It is larger than the firſt, for it is 220 miles acroſs, and lies under the equinoctial line. Regarding this ſecond lake very certain information is given by the Anzichi, near Congo, who trade in thoſe parts, and ſay there are people who ſail on the lake in large ſhips, and who write, and uſe weights and meaſures, ſuch as they have not in Congo, and that their houſes were built of ſtone and lime, and their cuſtoms reſembled thoſe of the Portugueſe. Hence it might be ſuppoſed the Empire of Preſter John was not far off. From this ſecond lake the Nile flows to the Iſland of Meroe a diſtance of 700 miles, other rivers running into it, the principal of which is the River Colves, ſo called becauſe it iſſues from a lake of that name on the borders of Melinde. When the Nile reaches Meroe it divides into two branches, and encompaſſes a high land, called Meroe, to the right of which on the eaſt, is a river named Abagni, which riſes in the Lake Bracina, and traverſes the Empire of Preſter John, till it reaches the aforeſaid iſland. On the weſtern ſide flow other rivers, one of which is the Saraboe.

The Nile, therefore, having received theſe rivers, and encircled that iſland, becomes again a ſtill larger ſtream, running through Ethiopia, (already ſpoken of as Egypt) as far as the falls, which are formed by a very high valley, that contracts here, and ſhuts the river into a narrow channel, from which the water pours down with terrific noiſe near the Iſland of Syene. From thence the Nile, after watering Egypt, diſcharges its waters into the Mediterranean directly over againſt the Iſland of Cyprus, by two principal branches, that on the eaſt at this preſent time being called Damiata, and that on the weſt Roſſetto. And, ſince we have come to the end of this hiſtory, with the Nile for our ſubject, it is a ſuitable place in which to ſum up the cauſe of its overflow. As we have narrated above, the chief cauſe of the riſe of the Nile is the great quantity of water poured down from the ſkies at the ſeaſon when winter commences in thoſe countries, and ſpring in our own parts, which, generally ſpeaking, is at the beginning of April. The rain does not fall there as it does in Europe, but copiouſly, and as it were by bucketſful inſtead of ſmall drops. Falling thus in torrents, the earth cannot drink it in, for, being ſteep and rocky, the water ruſhes with great force into the rivers, cauſing them to riſe, and ſwell, and overflow beyond all conception, particularly as the rains continue during the five months, of April, May, June, July, and Auguſt. The greateſt fall of rain, however, is in May, June, and July. Thus it happens, that the country having lofty mountains, and conſequently abounding in torrents, rivers, and lakes, theſe waters all meeting in the beds of great rivers, increaſe their ſize ſo as to make them larger than any others in the whole world. The Lakes alſo formed by them, as is ſeen in the sketch of the Cape of Good Hope and of Congo, and the ſurrounding kingdoms, are of ſuch marvellous ſize as to be called ſeas in thoſe regions.

And thus we ſee how the Nile in the above-mentioned ſeaſons ruſhes through thoſe countries northwards to water Egypt, the Rivers Zaire and Niger doing the ſame towards weſt and eaſt. Southwards are other very large rivers, which never fail to riſe at certain ſeaſons in like manner as the Nile. Now this occurs every year, but particularly at Cairo, and throughout Egypt, where the Nile begins to riſe about the end of June, and continues to do ſo till the 20th of September, as I myſelf have ſeen.

But the cauſe of ſuch overflow has up to the preſent time remained very obſcure, and although almoſt all the ancient writers, beginning at Homer, have left on record their belief that the riſe of the Nile was cauſed by the rains, nevertheleſs, they have not ſo diſtinctly declared it as does now Duarte Lopez, from having witneſſed it.

Some again aſſign its overflow to rains coming from the Mountains of the Moon, others to the melting of the ſnows on thoſe mountains, although the Nile does not riſe near the Mountains of the Moon, but a long way ſouth of them. Beſides, the winter ſeaſon brings ſnow itſelf, rather than heat to melt it.

Now I, having diligently inquired of Duarte Lopez concerning the above-mentioned matters, with certain previouſly formed deſigns, and he alſo himſelf propounding other ſubjects, like a man of high condition, which he is, and giving me ſuch anſwers as are ſet down in this diſcourſe, yet I feel aſſured that every one will not therewith be fully ſatiſfied or contented, and eſpecially the curious, the ſcientific, or thoſe ſkilled in matters of the world. The geographer would deſire to know more, and the phyſician, and the worker in metals, and the hiſtoriographer, and the merchant, and the mariner, and the preacher, with perhaps others differing from theſe in reſpect of their callings.

But Duarte Lopez promiſed to return with as great ſpeed as poſſible to Rome from Congo, whither he ſailed ſoon after he had furniſhed this account, which was in May of the year 1589, and to bring full information of what is lacking here touching the ſource of the Nile, and other matters. In the meantime, that which theſe leaves contain is by no means inſignificant; and if in them anything elſe ſhall be found that is uſeful, or ſtrange, or agreeable, or that drives away melancholy, let it be wholly aſcribed to the Moſt Noble and Very Reverend Monſignor Antonio Migliore, Biſhop of St. Mark, and Commander of the Order of the Holy Ghoſt, who has cauſed this work to be publiſhed for the public good.

Finis.

DEDICATION ON MAP OF AFRICA.

To the Moſt Illuſtrious and Moſt Reverend Monſignor Antonio Migliori, Biſhop of St. Mark, and Commander of the Order of the Holy Ghoſt.

Up to the preſent time there has been no ſuch correct repreſentation of Africa, of the Cape of Good Hope, of the Lakes, of the Nile, and of the Mountains from whence it flows, of the kingdoms of Preſter John, and of Congo and the ſurrounding countries, as that which our Duarte Lopez has furniſhed in his large Map, and which your Reverence has had reduced to this leſſer ſize. Now I confidently aſſert that in no printed Map of the preſent day is the true poſition of Egypt from Cairo ſouthwards ſo correctly ſhown as in this one, which (having twice travelled over the ſame ground) I have carefully arranged as far as the limited ſpace will allow. The places are denoted by letters on the little Chart placed above, by means of which the names may be attached to each.

From your Reverence's Servant,

FILIPPO PIGAFETTA.

From Rome, 2nd week of April, MDXCI.

"No Roſe without a Thorn."

DEDICATION ON MAP OF CONGO.

Filippo Pigafetta to the Moſt Illuſtrious and Moſt Reverend Monſignor Antonio Migliore, Biſhop of St. Mark and Commander of the Order of the Holy Ghoſt. Theſe deſcriptions and maps being chiefly deſigned to ſhow the ſituation of the Kingdom of Congo, which for lack of ſpace could not be included in the ordinary map of Africa brought from those countries by Duarte Lopez, we have engraved the ſaid kingdom on a ſeparate map on an enlarged ſcale, whereon are diſtinctly ſeen the Royal City and the other dependencies, the rivers, mountains, lakes, coaſts, harbours, and the boundaries of the countries of the Abyſſinians. There are alſo added the degrees of longitude according to Ptolemy, which were not on the other map, the Portugueſe geographers having no record of them. Nevertheleſs they are an extremely ingenious invention, for by means of them and of the degrees of latitude, without any other meaſurement, the diſtances between one place and another can be determined. We have alſo engraved the arms and ſeal of the King of Congo, adopted by him after the viſion we have recorded, it not being the cuſtom of thoſe kings, or of their nobles, to uſe as in Europe devices, or letters, or writing, or any other marks on their ſwords.

From Rome, 1591.

Pope Sixtus V., a magnanimous Prince, and born for the benefit of the Commonwealth, drove the thieves from the States of the Church. He placed four of the moſt perfect and remarkable obeliſks that were ever ſet up, on pedeſtals with a croſs on the top. He conſecrated the two Columns of Trajan and Antoninus, and ſet upon them the Images of St. Peter and St. Paul. He built two churches, and four

Papal palaces, and the Balcony of Benedictions, and the Holy Staircafe, and the Beggars' Hofpital, and the Vatican Library, and the wonderful Cupola of St. Peter. He brought the water called Aqua Felix into Rome by an aqueduct twenty miles in length, conveying it into fundry fountains, and ciſterns, and lavatoria, in the Efquiline, Quirinale, and Capitoline Hills. He beautified and reſtored the famous ſtatues made by Praxiteles and Phidias. He appointed twelve galleys for the ſafeguard of the Roman coaſt, and furniſhed the port of Civita Vecchia with water by a canal ſix miles long. He made five ſtraight ſtreets that lead to the principal churches of ancient Rome, by filling up valleys and levelling hills. He tranſferred the body of Pope Pius Quintus from St. Peter's to Santa Maria Maggiore, into a tomb he had himſelf ſet apart for it. He numbered amongſt the Doctors of the Church St. Bonaventura, and amongſt the Saints Didaco, a Spaniard, and a minor friar of the Obſervantes. He added three Biſhoprics to the Eccleſiaſtical Dominion, that of Loretto which he fortified with bulwarks, that of Montalto in his own country, and that of San Severino. He founded the School of Sciences at Fermo, and two Colleges—one in Bologna, called de Marchiani, and that of St. Bonaventura, in Rome. He raiſed the Tower of the Belvedere, and reſtored the church of St. Sabina. He built a fulling-houſe for the trade of wool. He collected together the treaſure of the See Apoſtolic for very neceſſity of famine, peſtilence, and war. Therefore, as Pope Sixtus IV. was accorded the title of Romulus, so is it fit that Sixtus V., who in the ſpace of five years wrought ſuch great matters, ſhould have that of Auguſtus, who, having found Rome made of brick, left it of marble. His intent was to perform other works but that it pleaſed the Lord God to call him to a better life; for he was minded—with materials all in readineſs—to make the

Flaminian Way meet by a bridge over the Tiber; and from the information given by this report he wiſhed to open the way and traffic to the Kingdom of Congo, and to the King of the Abyſſinians, called Preſter John, and by means of him to convert all Africa to Chriſtianity; and to put in execution divers other matters which are not here to be made mention of.

FILIPPO PIGAFETTA,

Natalis Bonifacius Incidebat.

MAP OF DUARTE LOPES.

"Map of Duarte Lopes."—"Suivant la dédicace à Antoine Migliori (25 avril 1591) de la carte de l'Afrique qui accompagne l'œuvre de Pigafetta, Duarte Lopes dreſſa une grande carte de '*l'Africa e il Capo de Buonna Speranza e il laghi del Nilo e il monti donde scende e il Reami de Prete Janni e di Congo e le contrade uicine*,' carte dont Pigafetta donne une réduction faite par ordre de Migliori. Sur cette réduction on voit au centre du continent et ſous l'Equateur un grand lac avec ſix îles, qui reçoit au S. une grande rivière à travers les contrées indiquées ſous le nomme de *Ambian* et *Cotia* (à l'E.) et de *Coda* et *Goyame* (à l'O.) ; cette rivière ſort d'un autre lac de la grandeur du premier à peu prés, ſituée ſous la même longitude et ſous le 12e parallèle auſtral, couvert également d'îles et peuplée d'hyppopotames, *cavalli marini*. Dans la partie méridionale de ce lac ſe jette, à ce qu'il parait, un cours d'eau qui ſemble être le premier tronçon de la rivière indiquée ; qui nait ſous la 22e parallèle S. entre des hautes montagnes, et qui a une ſource commune avec le fleuve *Manhice*. Ce fleuve ſe dirige vers l'océan indien et reçoit la rivière Bavagul, qui vient des montagnes du SO., terre de *Butva*. De ce même lac méridional deſcend le Zambeze ou *Cuama*. Avant d'arriver au lac central, cette première rivière, que par convention nous pourrions appeler le Lualaba de Lopes et qui dans ſon opinion eſt le Nil même, détache un bras qui va concourir à la formation du *Rio du Congo* (Zaire), lequel, par un autre bras, moins conſidérable, ſe relie à ce lac central. Le Zaïre reçoit du N. et du S. différents affluents, dont le plus important ſemble être celui qui vient d'un lac nommé *Aqueluna*, ſitué ſous le 11e parallèle auſtral. Ce lac communique avec le lac central-Sud, qui, d'un autre côté, donne également naiſſance au Quanza et au Dande, et qui, enfin, reçoit du S. un autre cours d'eau, qui vient d'un petit lac du pays de *Quinbebe*. Cet affluent, le plus important du Zaire, peut correſpondre au Kaſſabi des cartes modernes. En regardant cette partie de la carte, on croirait avoir ſous les yeux un deſſin groſſièrement tracé, mais aſſez reſſemblable, du Bemba, du Lualaba de Stanley et du Tanganyika, dans leur poſition relative et en mettant de côté les contours actuellement connus des lacs et les rapports aujourd'hui repouſſés par les géographes, du Lukuga. Du lac équatorial ou central ſ'élance dans la direction NE. le Nil ou mieux un bras du Nil, attendu qu'un autre cours d'eau, qui le rejoint au

10e parallèle N. nommé *Rio Golués* (qui a pour affluent le Tacaij), prend ſa ſource très à l'E. *sous l'équateur* et dans le lac Colue ; que un ſecond cours d'eau, qui le rejoint à la hauteur de Meroe, a également ſa ſource à l'E. ſous le 5e parallèle N. au lac Barcena, qui communique avec la mer par le *Rio de Jeila*,—et que, enfin, un troiſième bras vient de l'O. d'un lac également ſitué au N. du grand lac central, ſous le 11e parallèle N. Ainſi, le Nil, outre ſa ſource priſe dans le grand lac central, poſſède trois autres ſources dans trois lacs principaux ſitués entre l'Equateur et le 11e parallèle N.; de ces trois lacs le moyen eſt ſitué ſous la ligne équatoriale ainſi que le Victoria Nyanſa. Le Zaire très rapproché de l'Equateur, reçoit ſes eaux de la grande rivière qui vient du lac le plus méridional du centre de l'Afrique, et auſſi du grand lac équatorial, comme cela arriverait ſi le Lukuga moderne était un véritable fleuve (en conſidèrant le lac comme correspondant au Tanganyika), et cette rivière était le Lualaba."

"Voici encore quelques indications qui offrent, me parait-il, un certain intérêt.

"Près du confluent de la rivière que nous nommerons le Lualaba de Lopes avec le Zaire, sous le 1e parallèle austral, on trouve le mot *Uangué* ou *Vangué* (VANGVE) dont la prononciation portugaise ou italienne ſe rapproche ſingulièrement de *Nyangwe*, ſurtout ſi nous le faiſons précéder de la particule *n*, ce qui n'est pas une opération trop arbitraire.

"A l'extrémité méridional de l'Afrique, ſous le 27e parallèle ſe deſſine un petit lac deſigné ſous le mot *Gale* et qui pourrait raiſonnablement correſpondre au Ngame ou Ngmi des cartes modernes.

"Au nord de l'Equateur on trouve encore un ſyſtème hydrographique curieux. Un bras du Vieux Calabar prend ſa ſource dans un *Lac Noire* (*Lago Negro*) et l'on voit dans le baſſin un peu confus du Niger quatre autres lacs, dont l'un, ſitué ſous le 14e parallèle, près du baſſin du Nil, dont il eſt ſéparé par une haute chaîne de montagnes, ſe nomme *Lago da Nubia*, tandis qu'un ſecond, ſous le 19e parallèle porte le nom de *Lago Chinonde* et rappelle par ſa ſituation relative le *Tchad*."

"Le Zambèze, cela eſt certain, prend ſa ſource dans un lac méridional qui pourait correſpondre à notre lac encore peu connu, le Bembe (*Bangweole*), mais il reçoit du Sud et du Nord de nombreux et forts affluents, et, l'un des premiers, ſ'approche du fleuve qui vient du Sud vers ce lac et par conſéquent des affluents que ce fleuve recoit de l'Oueſt.

"Or il eſt néceſſaire de remarquer que l'étude de la région du Bangweolo, du Loanjwe, du Kafue, du Kobongo ou Cubango, &c., eſt encore en grande partie à faire, et que l'on ne peut affirmer que celle du haut Zambèze ſoit entièrement faite.

"De ce premier lac ſort, vers le Nord, une autre fleuve qui, ſe rencontrant avec le Zaire et avec le Nil, conſtitue certainement une communité d'origine entre ces deux fleuves et le Zambèze; mais d'un autre côté ce fleuve ſ'identifie avec le Nil ſeulement parcequ'il va ſe jeter dans le ſecond lac ou lac équatorial, d'où le Nil ſort vers le Nord. Il n'eſt pas hors de propos de rappeler que Livingſtone admettait l'identité du Lualaba avec le Nil. Enſuite le Nil ne naît pas ſeulement dans ce lac central; il naît auſſi de trois autres *nyansas* (j'emploie ce mot pour déſigner trois lacs importants). Donc cette liaiſon avec le lac central et, à cauſe de cette liaiſon, ſon identité avec le *Lualaba*, qui vient du S., n'eſt pas un facteur eſſentiel dans l'hydrographie du Nil de Lopes. Et tellement que ce même Nil qui vient du grand lac va ſe réunir à l'autre qui ſort du lac *Colue de Lopes* (il convient de diſtinguer, comme nous le verrons plus bas) ſitué à l'E. et également ſous l'équateur, formant avec lui une ſeule des trois grandes branches originaires du véritable Nil.

"Le Zaire, enfin, naît dans le grand lac central de l'équateur, mais d'un autre côté il eſt identique au *Lualaba* qui vient du S., ou plutôt celui-ci coincide avec lui avant d'entrer dans ce lac, ce qui ſignifie que la liaiſon du Zaire avec ce lac pouvait correſpondre au Lukuga, ſuivant l'hypothèſe de Cameron, tout en laiſſant ſubſiſter l'identité du *Lualaba* avec le Zaire, ſuivant les informations de Stanley. Sur les cartes plus haut indiquées, on ſ'achemine évidemment vers ce *desideratum* de l'hydrographie africaine de Lopes, et perſonne ne pourra nier que les révélations des explorations modernes ont avec cette hydrographie un rapport plus logique que ne l'ont certaines doctrines et hypothèſes enregiſtrées ſur des cartes de l'Afrique relativement récentes."—*L'Hydrographie Africaine, par M. Luciano Cordeiro*, p. 23—27.

THE CARTOGRAPHY OF AFRICA FROM 1492 TO 1600, AS ILLUSTRATIVE OF THE NOMENCLATURE OF THE CONGO.

The following is a liſt of upwards of thirty maps and globes, the originals of which were, for the moſt part, made during the 15th century. The initials refer to authors, the titles of whoſe works are given at the end of the Note:—

AUTHOR.	TITLE OF MAP OR GLOBE, AND REFERENCE.	PLACE.	DATE.	NAME OF RIVER.
1. Martin Behaim	Globe. B. H. J. K. M. S.	Nuremberg	1492	R. di Parto. Rio Pedoroso
2. Henrici Martelli	"FormaAffrice Secundum Descriptionem Portugalensium." Add MS. 15,760. S.	Brit. Mus.	c. 1495	Rio Poderoso. (Pota de Padron)
3. Juan de la Cosa	Mappemonde. H. J. S.	Madrid	1500	Rio del Padron
4. Johann Ruysch	Map in "Ptolemæi Geographia." S.	Rome	1508	Padron F.
5. Ptolemy	"Charta Marina," and two Charts of Africa, in Geography. S.	Argentorati	1513	Rio de Manicogo
6. Anonymous	Globe. J.	Frankfort-on-the-Main	1520	Manicongo
7. Fern.Columbus	Carta Universal, for Emp. Char. V. S.	Weimar	1527	Manicongo
8. Diego Ribero	Carta Universal ,,	Weimar and Rome	1529	R. de Manicongo
9. Oronce Finé	Orbis Descriptio, from Grynaeus, 1532	Paris	1531	R. Manicogo
10. Gerard Mercator	Globe	Louvain	1541	R. Manicongo
11. John Rotz	Portolano, 20 E IX. M.	Brit. Mus.	1542	Manicongue
12. SebastianCabot	Mappemonde. J.	Paris	1544	Monicongo
13. Pierre Desceliers	Mappemonde (Lord Crawford's Copy). M.	Made at Arque	1545	R. di Manicogue
14. Diogo Homem	Portolano (add. MS. 5415[a]). H. S.	Brit. Mus.	1558	R. de Manconguo
15. Ant. Florianus	Map of the World	Udine or Venice	c. 1560	R. de Manicongo
16. Ant. Sal[amanca]	Orbis Imaginem	Rome	c. 1560	R. de Manicogo
17. Paulo Forlani	Descrittione dell' Africa. (Map)	Venice	1562	Zaire F.
18. Giacomo Gastaldi	Large Map of Africa	Venice	1562	Zaire F.
19. Niccolo Nelli	Map of Africa	Venice	1564-5	Zaire F.
20. P. Cimerlini	Cosmographia Universalis	Verona	1566	R. Manicogo
21. J. Martines	Map of Africa. S.	Messina	1567	Manicongo
22. Gerard Mercator	Large Mappemonde. J.	Duisbourg	1569	Manicongo
23. Abraham Ortelius	Map of Africa in Theatrum	Antwerp	1570	Zaire
24. Fernao Vaz Dourado	Portolano (lamina 10)	Made at Goa. MS. B. Mus.	1573	Comgo
25. André Thevet	Africa in La Cosmographie Universelle	Paris	1575	Manicongue
26. Rumold Mercator	Map of World in Atlas	Antwerp	1587	Manicongo
27. M. Liv. Sanuto	Map of Africa, tab x. in Geografia	Venezia	1588	Zaires Fluvius
28. Johann Duetechum	Tabula Aphricæ	Deventer	1590	R. Zaire, R. de Manicongo Zaire Incolis
29. *Fil. Pigafetta*	*Tavola generale dell' Africa.* B. H. M.	*Rome*	1591	*Rio de Congo and Zaire*
30. ,,	*Tavola del Reame de Congo.* B. H. M.	*Rome*	1591	*Rio de Congo, Rio Zaire*
31. Petrus Plancius	Orbis Terrarum Typus	Amsterdam	1594	Zaire
32. A. F. a Langren	Typus. Manicongo and Angola	Amsterdam	1596	Rio de Manicongo, Zaire Incolis
33. Jodocus Hondius	Map of World. Drake and Cavendish	Amsterdam	1596	Manicongo
34. ,,	Typus Orbis Terrarum	Amsterdam	c. 1597	Zaire
35. E. Wright and Molyneux	Hydrographical Description, or "New Map"	London	1600	R. de Manicongo
36. J. Pory.	Map of Africa in Leo Africanus.	London.	1600	Zaire and Bancare.

AUTHORS QUOTED IN LIST OF MAPS.

(B.) Burton, Capt. R. F. "Gorilla Land and the Cataracts of the Congo," 1876.
(H.) Hutchinson, Edward. "The Lost Continent," 1879.
(J.) Jomard. "Monuments de la Geographie."
(K.) Kiepert, H. "Beitrage zur Entdeckungs-Geschichte Afrika's," 1873-4.
(M.) Major, R. H. "Prince Henry the Navigator," 1868.
(S.) Santarem. "Essai sur la Cosmographie" (Atlas), 1849.

I am indebted to Mr. C. H. Coote, of the Britiſh Muſeum, for the following exhauſtive note on this ſubject:—

The earlieſt document of any importance to our inquiry is, the celebrated globe of 1492, made by Martin Behaim, of Nuremburg, who accompanied Diego Cam in his firſt diſcovery of the Congo. The evidence afforded us by this and the three ſucceeding maps is, that the earlieſt name of this river was *not* the Congo, as ſtated by Burton, but either the "Rio de Padraõ," the River of the Pillar, or "Rio Podoroſo," the Mighty River, which laſt, to ſay the leaſt, is ſignificant. Behaim writes them thus: "R. di Parto," and "Rio Pedoroſo;" theſe, it is evident, are corruptions at the mouth of a German, of the names that are found on the contemporary map of c. 1495. On this laſt is to be ſeen the "Põta de Padron," the *point* on the ſouthern ſhore of the mighty river, where Diego Cam erected the pillar in 1484, as related by De Barros.

We obſerve for the firſt time on the maps or charts of 1513, the change of the name to "Rio de Manicongo," which held its own without intermiſſion upon ſubſequent maps, as a glance at the liſt will ſhow, down to 1560. This change we believe to be due to Spaniſh influence. Theſe maps of 1513 have been regarded by ſome as the actual work of the great Columbus, but a compariſon of them with the previous map of 1500, by Juan de la Coſa, the pilot of Columbus, does *not*, ſo far as the name of our river is concerned, favour the theory of a family reſemblance with the earlier map.

It will be convenient here to draw attention to a work which we believe has entirely eſcaped the notice of modern writers upon the Congo, Burton excepted. Not only is it the earlieſt book on geography printed in Spain, but it alſo may be regarded as the firſt book on navigation. It affords us one of the earlieſt, if not the earlieſt printed account of the river and Kingdom of Manicongo, which is as curious as it is intereſting. The book referred to is the "Suma de Geografia," by Martin Fernandez de Enciſo, publiſhed at Seville in 1519, fol. The mighty river is called here the "Rio de Manicongo," and to this book we attribute the maintenance of the name upon ſubſequent maps and works on geography for nearly half a century. Deſcribing the uſe of money in Manicongo, Enciſo writes: "En Manicongo vſan caracolicos por moneda: & aſſi cōprā & vēdē con ellos como noſtros cō la plata y el ora" (fol. v.).—*Trans.* In Manicongo they uſe ſhells for money, and alſo buy and ſell with them as we do with ſilver and gold.—For further facts relating to the author, his book, and its contents, we refer the reader to the valuable Bibliography of Navigation, which is appended to the "Voyages and Works of John Davis," edited for the Hakluyt Society, by Captain A. H. Markham, R.N., 1880, p. 345.

We now come to the name Zaire, which was firſt uſed by De Barros in his two firſt decades, publiſhed at Liſbon, in 1552. His uſe of the name exerciſed no influence over map-makers until ten years later. In 1561 theſe two decades were for the firſt time tranſlated into Italian, and publiſhed at Venice in 1562. The reſults of this tranſlation are ſhown in the Map of Forlani, the famous large Map of Africa by G. Gaſtaldi, publiſhed the ſame year, and in all the maps ſubſequently publiſhed in Venice down to the end of the century. It will be obſerved that this example was followed by the famous Abraham Ortelius, and nearly all of the geographers of the Low Countries, with the remarkable exceptions of the younger Mercator and Peter Plancius. Ortelius, in his African geography, avowedly followed De Barros and Ramuſio. The name of Pigafetta has been aſſociated with the Parergon of Ortelius, but upon what ground it is not quite clear. This much is clear, that he in no way modified the African geography of Ortelius.

According to the evidence afforded us by our liſt, the firſt to uſe the name Congo upon a map was not Pigafetta, as might be reaſonably ſuppoſed, but a fellow-countryman of Duarte Lopes, named Fernão Vaz Dourado, born at Goa, in the Eaſt Indies. In the beautiful Portolano made by him, we find the name Co*m*go uſed as early as 1573 (if not earlier, as this is only a copy), thereby anticipating its uſe by Pigafetta at leaſt eighteen years.

In the Geografia of M. Liv. Sanuto, Venice, 1588, we obſerve a reverſion to Zaires Fluvius, due to the tranſlation of Barros into Italian, as before mentioned.

We now arrive at the period of the appearance of the work of Pigafetta. All that is neceſſary to notice is, the uſe of two names, the Congo and the Zaire, on the map. In direct oppofition to Burton, we find Pigafetta applying the name Congo to the mouth and lower parts of the river, and the Zaire to the upper portion towards the equator. It has been ftated that in his geography Pigafetta found no fucceffor; this is hardly accurate. He found an imitator in Peter Plancius, in 1594, who not only gives the Zaire, but alfo the two equatorial lakes. This map is fometimes found in 17th century editions of Linfchotens' Voyages in Dutch.

In the map of 1600 we obferve a return to the old form of R. de Manicongo, which is due to Spanifh fources.

As we have feen, the influence of the geography of Pigafetta was only tranfient as fhown by the folitary example of Plancius. The book itfelf, however, has not been without its influence on Englifh literature, as witneffed in the "Voyages of Captain Singleton," written by the prince of ftory-tellers, Daniel Defoe.

"Tales of African Travel Three Hundred Years Ago," bafed upon an imperfect knowledge of Ortelius, and ftories of "Acrofs the Dark Continent in 1700," or "Stanley Anticipated," are, without a comparative ftudy of the old maps of the 15th and 16th centuries in their proper fequence, and fome knowledge of the text of our old friend Pigafetta, juft fo much idle fpeculation and gueff-work.

The queftion of the etymology of the name of the "Zaire," or "Nyadi," is beft left in the hands of Burton, Stanley, and others, who have at leaft fome knowledge of the languages of the countries bordering upon the "mighty river," Congo.—*C. H. Coote.*

In connexion with Mr. Coote's laft remark, it is worthy of notice that Stanley, in his defcent of the River Zaire, firft met with the name of Congo, in lat. 1° 40′ N., long. 21° 50′ E. He was kindly received, after various encounters with favages, by the chief, Rubunga; and he fays, "Before leaving the Chief of Rubunga's prefence, I afked him the name of the river, in a mongrel mixture of Ki-Swahili, Kinyamwezi, Kijiji, Kiregga, and Ki-Kufu. He underftood after a while, and replied, it was 'Ibari.' But after he had quite comprehended the drift of the queftion, he replied in a fonorous voice, 'Ikatu ya Kongo.'"—*Through the Dark Continent*, p. 283.—*Tr.*

Merolla, who went to Congo in 1682, fays, in referring to that region, —"Hence, in confequence of its (Zaire) waters being fomewhat yellow, the river is known for a hundred miles as it flows into the fea, and by means of it many large kingdoms were difcovered, hitherto unknown.

For the King of Portugal, Don Juan II., having ſent a fleet of ſhips, under Diego Cam, to this ſouthern coaſt of Africa, that experienced admiral conjectured he was near land from the waters of the Zaire. After entering it, he aſked the negroes what river and country it was, who replied, as if not underſtanding him, "Zevoco," which, in the Congoean tongue, is as much as to ſay, "I don't know," and from thence, through a corruption the name is called Zaire.—*Viaggio nel regno di Congo*, p. 48.

Alli o mui grande reino está de Congo,
Por nós ja convertido á fé de Christo,
Por onde o Zaire passe claro e longo,
Rio pelos antiguos nunca visto.

Lusiads of Camoens, canto v. 13.

That lucid river, the long-winding Zaire,
Flood which the roving ancients never saw,
Through Congo runs, a realm extending far,
Where erst our nation sow'd the Christian law.

Quillinan.

BIBLIOGRAPHICAL NOTE UPON THE 16TH-CENTURY EDITIONS OF PIGAFETTA.

It has been thought that the appearance of the preſent tranſlation would be none the leſs welcome if accompanied by a ſhort notice of the labours of others in this direction. We therefore append, for the guidance of thoſe who may be intereſted in the ſubject, a bibliographical note of the firſt four 16th-century editions of Pigafetta, as ſhowing the eſtimation in which our author's narrative was held by his cotemporaries at this moſt intereſting period in the hiſtory of geography. This appreciation can only be fully realized by an examination of the ſumptuous 4th edition by the brothers De Bry, of 1597, in German. The title-page, maps, and plates are maſterpieces of the engraver's art, and ought to be better known. They are ſuperior to, and more in number than, the originals done in Rome.

BIBLIOGRAPHY OF PIGAFETTA.

I. Relatione del Reame di Congo et delle circonvicine contrade tratta dalli Scritti & ragionamente di Odoardo Lopez Portogheſe per Filippo Pigafetta con diſſegni vari di Geografia, di piante, d' habiti, d' animali & altro. Al molto Ill$^{re.}$ & R$^{mo.}$ Mons$^{re.}$ Antonio Migliore Veſcouo di S. Marco, & Commendatore di S. Spirito.

In Roma Appreſſo Bartolemeo Graſſi (1591. 4to).

Collation. Title-page engraved, surmounted with the arms of Migliore, dedication and tavola del capitoli, 3 leaves, text of 83 pp.

Maps. 1. "Il dissegno dell' Africa :" t. r., arms of, and dedication to Sixtus V.; b. r., arms of Migliore, with dedication to same; below, arms of Pigafetta. Size 25 in. × 17½.

2. "Tavola del Regno di Congo :" b. l., arms of 1st King of Congo, Sixtus V., and Migliore, with dedication to latter; below, arms of Pigafetta with his motto, "Il n'est rose sans espine." 17 in. × 20.

Plates.—1. Spetie di Palma. 2. Zebra. 3. Habito del Nobile. 4. Habito del Soldato. 5. Habito dell donna. 6. Modo di far Viaggio. 7. Atro modo d' andar attorno. 8. Atro modo d' andar in posta; each 8 in. × 11¾.

Three examples in Brit. Mus., Grcn. Lib. 7151. 566. e. 20. 146. b. 4; the last imperfect, "dissegno dell' Africa" wanting.

II. De beſſchryvinghe vant groot ende vermaert Coninckrijck van Congo, ende de aenpalende oft ommegheleghen Landen, mit verclaringhe van veel ſonderlinghe ſaken ende gheſchiedeniſſen van den ſelfden Coninckrijcke. Ghenomen wt de ſchriften ende mondelicke t' ſamen ſpraecken, van Edoart Lopez, Portegijs.

Beſchreven door Philips Pigafetta in Italiaens, ende overgheſet in ons Nederlantſche ſpraecke: Deur Martijn Everart-B.

(*Description of the great and celebrated Kingdom of Congo, and of the surrounding countries, with the explanation of many things and singular histories touching the same kingdom. Taken from the writings and discourses of Edward Lopez, Portuguese.*

Written in Italian by Philip Pigafetta, and translated into Dutch by Martin Everart B.(*ruges*)

t'Amſtelredam, by Cornelis Claeſz. Opt Water int Schrijſboeck, by De Oude Bruggh. M.D.XCVI. 4to.

Collation. Map of Congo, by Jodocus Hondius, on title-page; neither dedication or pagination. Plates reduced and inserted in text; Zebra (2) omitted.

Note.—Curious as being the first translation of Pigafetta, but of no real value. Everart was a well-known translator into Dutch of early Spanish works on Navigation.

III. A Report of the Kingdom of Congo, a Region of Africa, and of the Countries that border round about the ſame, &c.

Drawn out of the writings and diſcourſes of Odoardo Lopez, a Portingall, by Philippo Pigafetta. Tranſlated out of Italian by Abraham Hartwell.

London: printed by John Wolfe, 1597. 4to. Title in duplicate.

Collation. Verso of first title-page, arms of John Whitgift, Archbishop of Canterbury. Dedication to the same, 5 pp. "Translator to the Reader," 11 pp. text, 217 pp.; and table, 3 pp.

Maps. 1. Map of Africa: t. r., arms of Sixtus V., in place of dedication, explanation of map; b. r., arms of Pigafetta. 2. "A Mappe of the Kingdome of Congo," t. r., arms of first King of Congo; b. l., dedication to Sixtus V., translated and transposed (cf. No. 1 of original).

These two rare maps were executed by William Rogers, one of the earliest known English engravers. The eight plates are rough reduced wood engravings from the originals.

IV. Regnum Congo hoc eſt Warhaffte und Eigentliche Beſchreibung deſz Königreichs Congo in Africa, und deren angrentzenden Länder, darinnen der Inwohner, Glaub, Leben, Sitten vnd Kleydung wol und auſzführlich vermeldet vnd angezeigt wirdt.

Erſtlich durch Eduart Lopez, welcher in dieſer Navigation alles Perſönlich erfahren, in Portugaleſiſcher Spraach geſtellt, Jetzo aber in vnſer Teutſche Spraach tranſferieret vnd vberſetzt durch Auguſtinum Caſſiodorum.

Auch mit ſchönen und Kunſtrichen Figuren gezieret und an Tag geben durch Hans Dietherich und Hans Iſrael von Bry Gebrüder und Bürger zu Franckfurt.

Getruckt zu Frankfort (*sic*) am Mayn durch Johan Saur. . . Im Jahr M.D.XCVII. Fol.

(*A true and correct description of the Kingdom of Congo, in Africa, and the adjoining territories, in which the religion, mode of life, customs and dress of the inhabitants are fully set out. First put forth in the Portuguese language by Edward Lopez, who learned all personally in this navigation, but now translated and published in the German language by Augustine Cassio.*

Also adorned with beautiful and artistic figures, and set forth by John Theodore and John Israel De Bry, brothers, and citizens of Frankfort. Painted at Frankfort-on-the-Mayn by John Sauer, M.D.XCVII. Fol.)

This edition of Pigafetta forms the firſt part of the famous "Petits Voyages of De Bry." (M. Sobolewſki's ſet of the "Grands et Petits Voyages," of 55 vols., was ſold for 19,000 fr. (£750).)

Collation. 73 pp. Maps, copies of originals without dedications. 1. Africa: t. r., two cartouches blank; b. r., description of map beginning, "Tabulam hanc Aegypti." 2. "Tabula Geogra Regni Congo:" b. l., arms of 1st King of Congo, and Migliore, with address to reader, within cartouch.

Plates. The great interest attached to this edition is, that it has six more plates than the first. Plates 4 to 10 are copied from the originals, the remainder are seven plates, ubiquitously illustrative of various scenes in the narrative. Plate 1 shows the first landing of the Portuguese at the mouth of the Congo, the building of the first church, and the baptism of the Mani Sogno and his son. Plate 11 is as ludicrous as it is beautifully executed. The engraving of the maps and plates is superior to the original. In this edition the narrative of Pigafetta reached the zenith of its fame, in the 16th century. It has not received the attention it deserves. Example in Brit. Mus., Gren. Lib. $\frac{6607}{1}$. See also Catalogue of the Huth Library, vol. ii. p. 440.

It was republished in Latin in the following year (1598). Second German Edition, 1609; Second Latin Edition, 1624.

The only remaining tranſlations that call for notice are those of Linſchoten (1598), and Purchas (1617-25), Part 2. The latter is a reprint from Hartwell, with the map by Hondius inſerted (cf. 2nd edition of 1596). Theſe have been copied more or leſs correctly in the various ſubſequent "Collections of Voyages and Travels," down to our day.

NOTES.

(P. 21) "AMBER."—This is evidently a confufion of names, and here means Ambergris, or Grey Amber, which is now known to be a morbid fecretion formed in the inteftines of the fpermaceti whale, and is found floating upon the fea, on the fea-coaft, or in the fand near the fea-coaft. It is met with in the Atlantic Ocean, alfo on the Coaft of Africa. There are curious early legends in the pages of Olaus Magnus, regarding the Ambergris found floating on the North Sea.—*Tr.*

(P. 23) "AMBIZE ANGULO."—Merolla, a Capuchin prieft, who gives an account of the Kingdom of Congo in 1682, ftates that all through the River Zaire is found the "Pefce Donna," which has a refemblance to the human form. His defcription of its appearance and habits feems to identify it with the "Ambize Angulo" of Pigafetta. *John Ogilby* fays, that by the inhabitants it is called Ambis Angalo, but by the Europeans, Meremen, and Meremaids. This fifh is probably the creature known as the Manatee, which is found in the rivers of the Weft African Coaft. Its refemblance to the human form is not a Portuguefe ftory, for the fame defcription is given of it by the natives at the prefent time. In the account of the afcent of the River Binué by the "Henry Venn" Miffion fteamer, as narrated in Petermann's Mittheilungen for May, 1880, is the following defcription of the capture of the Manatee: "Zwei Tage vor unferer Ankunft auf der Rückreife war hier ein Ajú (Manatus Vogellii) gefangen worden, deffen Schädel der Leiter unferer Expedition aus dem Dunkel des Fetifchhaufes erlöfte. Von diefem Thiere geht am Niger wie am Benuë die Sage, dafs es einen ganz menfchgleichen Kopf und zwei volle runde Brüfte habe. Defhalb auch müffte erfterer fofort abgefchnitten und vergraben oder dem Fetifch gewecht werden, weil niemand, der den Kopf gefehen, das Fleifch des Thieres effen würde."—*Tr.*

"We proceeded on our voyage up the River Coanza, which is deep and rapid, and abounds with crocodiles, alfo the hippopotamus and phoca—which the people call Peixe Mulher, or fifh-woman—which is an amphibious, cetaceous animal, very harmlefs. It grazes along the banks of the river without leaving the water; it is from feven to eight feet long, with two fmall paws or feet, between which there are two large teats. There is a certain bone of this animal to which the people afcribe great medicinal virtue; from its hide are made the whips wherewith the flave-drivers flog the unfortunate flaves."—*Six Years in W. Africa, by F. T. Valdez*, p. 131.

(P. 18) "ANGOLA."—On devrait écrire *Ngola* ou *NGola.* La cour du roi d'Angola était primitivement *Loanda* (plutôt: *Luanda*, de *luanda;* partie baffe) mais à la fuite de l'invafion portugaife elle fe tranfporta à l'endroit où eft aujourd'hui le fort de *Pongo-andongo* (*Pungu-â-ndongo*, de *Pungu:* grande idole, et *ndongo:* grand village) dont il eft réfulté que cet endroit a pris le nom de *Cabanza* ou *NBanza-ia-cabaça*, c'eft-à-dire: *seconde cour*, feconde réfidence, ou feconde *NBanza* (*Cabaça* eft une corruption de *Cabanza*). L'ancienne cour de Luanda était appelée: *NBanza-ia-Caculu* (*Caculu:* premier; *Cabanza* ou *Cabaça:* fecond).—*Vid. Ann. do. Cons. Ultr.* art. *Angola. Obs. de J. V. Carneiro*, 1861, fec. ii.

(P. 39) "ANGOLA NEGROES."—They would laugh to fcorn our military expeditions, were it not for our field-pieces, of which they ftand in great fear. During our war with the interior, in 1787, I saw 17 men and a field-piece put to flight the Sova of Quiaca and his 12,000 negroes, who dropped all the loot which they had juft taken from the Cobaes.—*Lands of Cazembe*, p. 26.

(P. 26) "ANZICHI AND ANZICANA."—En parlant du premier établiffement définitif des Portugais au Congo, *Barros* f'était rapporté à une révolte des peuples du lac *d'où sort le Zaire*, et avait affuré que quelques Portugais accompagnèrent le roi Africain dans fa marche contre ce peuples. L'illuftre chroniqueur avait dit auparavant: "Et attendu que prefque lors de l'arrivée des notres parvint au roi (du Congo) la nouvelle que les peuples Mundequetes qui habitent près *d'un grand lac d'ou sort le Zaire*, qui parcourt toute cette contrée, f'étaient révoltés." "Il nous apprend également, et Refende, auffi, que quelques Portugais accompagnèrent cette expedition contre les Sufdits Mundequetes, ou plutôt contre les *Anzikos.* Cette campagne avait été déjà racontée par *Garcia de Resende* qui difait fimplement que les peuples révoltés étaient des "Vaffaux du Roi du Congo qui lui défobéiffaient, et qui habitaient *quelques îles Situées sur le Rio do Padrão.*"—*Lyvro das obras de Garcia Resende*, I^me^ Ed. 1536. Il eft à remarquer dès à préfent que l'objection de *Lopes* me femble évidemment née d'un quiproquo, et qu'il fe rapportait au lac le plus méridional, tandis que

Barros faifait naturellement allufion au lac central, puifque *Lopes* avoue que les *Anzicos* révoltés habitaient au deffus de la cataract les deux rives du Zaire, jufqu'au lac appartinenti al ré di Congo, et qu'il ajoute "Hor quefto fiume, &c." Les renfeignements rélatifs à ces *Anzikos* font très curieux. Suivant l'opinion générale ce pays des *Anzikos* ou *Anzicana*, Nteka ou Grande-Angeka, fuivant d'autres, eft le pays de *Mikoko* ou *Makolo* (à la confluence du Nyali ou *Mikoko Sala*), et fa ville principale *Monsul* eft, fuivant Drapper à 300 lieues de la côte. Stanley dit que *Anzico*, *Monsul*, *Concobella* et autres dénominations locales des cartes (*anglaises*) font inconnues des indigènes qu'il a interrogés, mais que *Monsul* peut correfpondre à *Mossul* (ou *Little River*) ainfi nommé par les indigènes. Le fait n'a rien d'extraordinaire et ne détruit pas les renfeignements directs et pofitifs que nous poffédons depuis le commencement du XVIe fiècle au fujet des *Anzikos*. Il ne faut pas croire cependant que *Lopes* foit le premier qui ait parlé de ce peuple étrange : déjà au commencement du XVIe fiècle *Duarte Pacheco* difait que au N.E. du Congo fort avant dans l'intérieur, on connaiffait une contrée nommée *Anzica* habitée par des noirs comme ceux du Congo, mais antropophages et qui fe marquaient le front de deffins en fpirales.—*MS. Esmeraldo de situ orbis* (1505), à la Bibl. de Lisbonne. Serait-ce une trop grande audace que de voir dans ces peuples les ancêtres de ces féroces guerriers qui, à la hauteur du I° de lat. N. où vient déboucher du côte du N. un large fleuve que Stanley croit être le Welle de Schweinfurth, attaquèrent la valareufe expédition Anglo-Americaine ou, ne ferait-elle, la notre *Anzica* la *Nganza* de Stanley? Que l'on compare le récit de Lopes en 1591 avec celui de l'héroique explorateur du Zaire en 1877.—*M. Luciano Cordeiro, L'Hydrographie Africaine*, pp. 12, 54, 57.

(P. 26) "Aquilaria Agallocha."—(Aloes-wood tree—Black Agallocha—Eagle-wood tree—Agila-wood tree—as English synonyms). Defcribed by Roxburgh as an immenfe tree, a native of mountainous tracts, E. and S.E. of Sylhet, in lat. 24° to 25° N. Supposed to be one of the trees that furnifh the eagle-wood of commerce.—*Fancy Woods of India*, p. 35, *Ed. Balfour*, *Madras*, 1862.

(P. 49) "Bada."—The Abada is called by the Africans Pembére, and by the Portuguefe Unicorn.

(P. 116) "Bay of Lourenço Marques."—Cette baie fut découverte par nous avant 1506; déjà au temps de *Barros* (1552) et de *Mesquita*

Prestrello (1554) le nom de "*rio da lagoa*" donné au fleuve de l'Espirito Santo (Saint Esprit) que les Anglais nomment *English River* (?) depuis 1823, était regardé comme ancien, mais soit sur la carte de *Ribero* (1529) soit sur celle de *Diogo Homem* (1558) et bien aussi sur d'autres cartes encore, *l'ancien* nom qui répresentait les prémiers renseignements obtenus au sujet de la naissance de ce fleuve dans un lac intérieur :—*Alagoa Grande*, est conservé à la baie.—*L. Cordeiro*, p. 46. Il faut distinguer les deux faits de la *découverte* et de *l'exploration* pour ne pas attribuer à Lourenço Marques la découverte que d'autres Portugais en firent avant lui. . . . La découverte en doit avoir eu lieu entre le premier voyage de Vasco da Gama (1497) et l'année 1506 (voyage de *Barbudo* et *Quaresma*) *Baie de L. Marques.—Question entre le Portugal et la Gr. Bretagne.—Première Mémoire*, 1873.

(P. 44) "BEMBE."—The mines of Bembe were given to the Portuguese by the King of Congo towards the end of the 16th century. These mines remained unattended to till 1855, when the King of Portugal established the præsidium of Pedro V., and gave instructions for the working of the mines. The malachite found in them is of superior quality and great beauty.—*F. T. Valdez*, p. 81.

(P. 41) "CABO NEGRO."—Here Bartholomew Diaz placed his second Padrão, or Memorial Pillar. It was in lat. S. 15° 40′ 42″, and long. E. (Greenwich) 11° 53′ 20″, between Mossamedes or Little Fish Bay, the Bissungo Bitlolo of the natives, to the north (S. lat. 15° 13′), and Great Fish Bay to the south (S. lat. 16° 30′ 12″).

Not many years ago, there stood, at Cape Negro, a column of jasper, having on it the national arms of Portugal. In the year 1786, Sir H. Popham and Captain Thomson, being appointed to examine the West Coast of Africa, state that they found a marble cross, near to Angra Pequena, lat. 26° 37′, on which were the arms of Portugal. This they rightly supposed to be one of the ancient Pedrões.—*F. T. Valdez*, p. 91.

(P. 18) "CADIZ."—Gadeira, or Gades. Strabo quotes Polybius, who relates that there is a spring within the Temple of Hercules at Gades, having a descent of a few steps to fresh water, which is affected in a manner the reverse of the sea-tides, subsiding at the flow of the tide, and springing at the ebb.—*Strabo. Bohn's C. Library*, page 258.

(P. 28) "CANNIBALS."—Cannibals all, especially the savage Ganguelas (a large tribe between the Gango River, a southern branch of the

Coanza of St. Paulo de Loanda, and the Cubango), they devour thofe ſlain in their ceafelefs, caufelefs wars; they kill for food the old and valuelefs captives, whilſt the young are carefully preſerved for ſale.—*Lands of Cazembe*, p. 17.

"CONGO."—Congo was diſcovered by Diego Cam, probably in 1484. He erected a ſtone pillar at the mouth of the river, which accordingly took the title of Rio de Padrão, and eſtabliſhed friendly relations with the natives, who reported the country was ſubject to a great monarch, Mwani Congo, or Lord of Congo, reſident at Ambaſſe, Congo. The Portugueſe were not long in making themſelves influential in the country. Goncalo de Souſa was deſpatched on a formal embaſſy in 1490, and the firſt miſſionaries entered the country in his train. The religion, if ſuch it can be called, of the Congoeſe is a groſs fetiſhism, and almoſt the only trace of their former Chriſtianization is the ſuperſtitious value attached to ſome ſtray crucifix, now employed as a charm. Circumciſion is practiſed by all the tribes. Polygamy prevails, every man having wives according to his wealth and rank. The coſtume of the men and women varies conſiderably with rank and the degree of European influence, but in general it is very ſlight. The climate of Congo is, in compariſon with that of moſt tropical countries, remarkably cool and agreeable. In the hot ſeaſon, the thermometer is ſeldom more than from 80° to 86° Fahrenheit in the ſhade, and in the "Cacimbo," or cool ſeaſon, it uſually ranges from 60° during the night, to 75° during the day. This low temperature is principally due to the weſterly breeze, which ſets in from the Atlantic about nine or ten o'clock in the morning, and continues blowing, not unfrequently with conſiderable violence, till after ſunſet.—*Encly. Brit.*, Ed. ix., vol. vi., p. 266.

(P. 25) "DANT."—Dant or Lant in zoology, called by the Africans Lampt, is an animal of the figure of a ſmall ox, but having ſhort legs. It has black horns, which bend round, and are ſmooth. Its hair is whitiſh, and its hoofs are black and cloven. It is ſo ſwift that no animal except the Barbary horſe can overtake it. Theſe dants are common in the deſerts of Numidia and Libya, and ſeveral northern provinces of Africa. Buffon ſuppoſes that this animal is the ſame with the dwarf ox or zebu. —*Rees' Cyclo.* vol. ii. D. Face rather narrow, forehead very flat, with the horns on the ſide of the high occipital ridge; withers with a ſmall but diſtinct hump. It is the *Bos elegans et parvus Africanus* of Belon; *Juvenca Sylveſtris* of Alpinus; *Bos Bubacus Africanus* of Brisson; *Salam Buffalo*, *Dwarf Bull*, and *Egyptian Zebu*, of various writers.—*Knight's Eng. Cyc. Nat. Hist.* vol. i. page 621. Two ſkulls from the Gambia were preſented to the Britiſh Muſeum by the late Lord Derby. A white male was in the Zoological Gardens, London, in 1850. Purchas deſcribes them (ii. 1002) as yellow.—*Tr.*

(P. 33) "DIAZ DE NOVAES, PAULO."—This man was grandſon to the famous Bartolomeo Diaz, who diſcovered the greater part of the Weſt Coaſt of Africa, and the Cape of Good Hope.

(P. 9) "DRAKE AND CAVENDISH."—With reference to the hatred naturally enough ſhown towards theſe two Engliſh heroes by Spaniſh and Portugueſe, Abraham Hartwell, the firſt tranſlator, in his ſomewhat pedantic addreſs to the Reader, has the following: "Among others that made theſe motions unto me, one there was, who being a curious and a diligent ſearcher and obſerver of Forreine adventures and adventurers, as by his good paines appeareth, came unto me, and preſently preſented me with this Portingale Pilgrime lately come to him out of the Kingdom of Congo, and apparrelled in an Italian veſture: intreating me very earneſtly that I would take him with me, and make him Engliſh: for he could report many pleaſant matters that he ſaw in his pilgrimage, which are indeed uncouth and almoſt incredible to this part of Europe. But within two houres conference, I found him nibbling at two moſt honourable gentlemen of England, whom in plaine tearmes he called Pirates: so that I had much ado to hold my hands from renting of him into many mo (ſic) peeces, then his Coſen Lopez the Doctor was quartered. Yet, my ſecond wits ſtayed me, and adviſed me, that I ſhould peruſe all his Report, before I would proceede to execution: which indeed I did. And, becauſe I ſaw that in all the reſt of his behaviour hee conteyned himſelfe very well and honeſtly, and that he uſed this lewd ſpeech, not altogether *ex amino*, but rather *ex vitio gentis*, of the now inveterate hatred, which the Spanyard and Portingale beare againſt our nation, I was ſo bold as to pardon him, and ſo taught him to ſpeake the Engliſh toung." This "Coſen" was no other than Dr. Roderigo Lopez, private phyſician to Queen Elizabeth, who was hanged and *quartered* at Tyburn, in 1593. The evidence for the relationſhip reſts wholly with Hartwell, who, probably, did not intend it to be taken literally. This day, June 7th, 1593, Lopus (*sic*) was executed, and two Portugals more, at Tyborne.—*Royal Commission of Historical MSS*., *7th Report*, *Appen*., p. 253.—*Tr.*

It is intereſting to learn from this addreſs to the Reader that the "diligent ſearcher and obſerver of Forreine adventures and adventurers" was Hakluyt. I am informed by Mr. C. H. Coote, of the Britiſh Muſeum, that he has ſucceeded in tracing the parentage of Hakluyt. He belonged to a family of Welsh extraction, not Dutch, as has been ſupposed.—See *Encyc. Brit.* page 378, *sub voce.*—*Tr.*

(P. 5) "DUARTE LOPEZ."—In the note on Pope Sixtus V. will be found mention of one Lopez, who, being at Rome at the very period when Duarte Lopez arrived there, it is more than pardonable to indulge in the thought that he may have owed, in part, his introduction to the Pope to his nameſake, if not his relative. Anyhow, the coincidence of time and name is too ſtriking to paſs over in ſilence.—*Tr.*

(P. 25) "EMPACHAS."—The fierce wild cattle which extend down the Weſt Coaſt of Africa. Paul du Chaillu brought home a ſpecimen from the Gaboon, where it is called the Nyare. Mr. Cooley (*Inner Africa laid Open*, p. 47) tranſlates it "Gnu," which is locally called Nhumbo.—*Lands of Cazembe*, p. 25, n.

(P. 52) "EMPALANGA."—This is a great beaſt like an ox, having two horns, and very ſavoury. They are of ſeveral colours, ſome brown, others red, and ſome white.—*John Ogilby*, *Africa*, page 530.

(P. 114) "GALE."—Sur la carte de Duarte Lopes à l'extrémité méridional de l'Afrique, sous le 27e parallèle se deſſine un petit lac deſigné ſous le mot *Gale* et qui pourrait raiſonnablement correſpondre au Ngame ou Ngmi des cartes modernes."—*M. L. Cordeiro*, page 25.

(P. 1) "HOLY GHOST, HOSPITAL OF THE."—This hoſpital is the oldeſt and largeſt in Rome. It is ſituate on the right bank of the Tiber, not far from St. Peter's, on the ſite of an earlier hoſpital built by Ina, King of the Saxons in 717; thence its name in Saſſia or Saxia. Erected by Innocent III. in 1207, it attained its preſent impoſing dimenſions on both ſides of the Borgo S. Spirito, through the foſtering care of ſucceeding Pontiffs down to the time of Pius VII., c. 1818.

The high altar in the chapel is by Palladio, and is the only genuine ſpecimen of his architecture to be found in Rome.

Attached to the hoſpital is the famous collection of ſurgical inſtruments and library bequeathed by the celebrated phyſician, J. M. Lanciſi.

Since the ſuppreſſion of the Order of the Holy Ghoſt in Rome in 1847, the ſeveral ſections of the hoſpital have been ſerved by medical ſtudents and ſiſters of mercy, under the direction of doctors and profeſſors attached to the Univerſity.—*Donovan's Rome*, vol. iii. page 839, and *Nibby's Itineraire de Rome*, 1876, page 333.

(P. 1) "HOLY GHOST, ORDER OF THE."—This order of *Hospitallers* muſt not be confounded with the two orders of *Chivalry* of the ſame name. (The firſt, founded by Louis d'Anjou in 1352, the ſecond by Henry III. of France, in 1578.—See *Larousse*, *Grand Dict.* vol. xiv. page 65.)

The order with which we have to do, is that of the *Hospitallers* of the Holy Ghoſt inſtituted by Innocent III. in 1207, aided by Gui or Guido, the founder of the parent order of Montpellier in France in 1195. Guido was the firſt Commendatore of the Hoſpital in Rome, from which place the affairs of the order were directed. At leaſt ten of theſe hoſpitals were to be found in Italy, ſix in France, three in Poland; they were alſo to be found in Germany, Spain, and the Indies.

As was uſual with theſe and other Hoſpitallers and Templars, they followed the rule of St. Auſtin, their clergy not being Monks, but Canons Regular. At a later period the Commendatore was generally an eccleſiaſtic. The office has produced one Pope, ſeven or eight Cardinals, two Archbiſhops, and twelve Biſhops. Antonio Migliore was the 47th Commendatore of the order. He had previouſly held the office of "Cappelano" to Sixtus V.—See *Abbé Migne*, *Encyclopédie Théologique*, tome xx., pages 202—222. The office of Commendatore of the Holy Ghoſt, as has been well ſaid, is now much like the Abbot of Glaſtonbury, "a remembrance," but hardly a hope, as the community was ſuppreſſed by Pius IX. in 1847.—*Tr.*

(P. 96) "JAGGAS."—Nos auteurs conſervent la tradition d'une grande invaſion ou d'une ſuite d'invaſions, dont l'une pendant la première moitié du XVIe ſiècle, de peuples très barbares et antropophages venus de l'intérieur de l'Afrique et qui étendirent leur domination juſqu'à Gambia et au Congo. Ces peuples étaient, ſuivant Almada (1594) les *Mandimanças* ou plutôt les *Manes* plus connus ſous le nom de *Sumbas.*

Dans la *Rélation ann.* des Jésuites (Guinée) relative à 1602—1605 (Ed. de 1605) il eſt dit que ces envahiſſeurs ſ'appelaient au Congo *Iacás*, à Angola *Gindas*, dans l'Inde (?) *Zimbas*, dans l'Ethiopie du Prête, *Gallas*, et dans la Guinée, *Cumbas* "nom qui fut changé en celui de *Manes*" qui parvint juſqu'à *Serra Leoa* (Sierra Leone.)

Almada (1594) ſuppoſe que le nom de *Mandi* vient des *Mandingas*, celui de *Casa*, des *Casanges*, &c. Dans une autre occaſion je réunirai quelques données concernant cet important ſujet. Ce qui eſt certain, c'eſt qu'au temps d'Almada le *Mandi-mansa* était l'un des plus grands, ſinon le plus grand potentat du continent Africain à l'O. et au N. du Congo. *Mansa* en langage *Mandinga* ſerait, parait-il, l'équivalent de *Muene* dans celui du Congo. De là *Mandi-mansa*, maître, roi, empereur. Ce Mani-manſa eſt, ſans doute, le *Musameli* de Leardus (1448).—*M. L. Cordeiro*, p. 9.

(P. 30) "LAGO ACHELUNDA."—D'où part un affluent du Zaire qui eſt peut-être le Kaſſabi ou le Guango des cartes modernes.—*L. Cordeiro*, Note, p. 52.

(P. 44) "LIBATA."—The Libata, or Libatta, is a ſmall, the Banza a large village; the Cubata is a ſingle hut.—Burton's *Lands of Cazembe*, p. 17, n.

(P. 67) "LUCO."—I can only ſuggeſt that Luco or Moſango means either the *Pennisetum*, or the Eaſt Indian Nagli or Nanchni (in Portuguese Naxerim), the Arabic Dukhun, the Kisawahili Uwimbi (*Eleusine Coaracano*). Maize is locally known to the Portuguese as "Milho Burro."—*Lands of Cazembe*, p. 17, n.

(P. 19) "LUMACHE."—From Limax, a ſnail. The native name is Simbo.—John Ogilby, Maſter of the Revels to Charles II., thus deſcribes the Simbo or Cowrie: "Simbos, or little horn ſhells, are of two kinds in Angola, and ſerve in lieu of money. Pure ſimbos are found near the Iſland of Loanda, and others, called Brazil, and brought from Rio de Janeiro, are uſed in Congo and Pinda, and alſo among the Jagas. The ſimbos of Loanda are alſo of two ſorts, a finer and a coarſer, which are ſeparated by ſifting. The latter are called Simbos Siſados, the other Fonda and Bomba. Both kinds are ſent to Congo in ſacks made of ſtraw, each ſack weighing two Arobas, that is, threeſcore and four pounds."—Burton ſtates that the Arabs call the Simbo, Kaure, and gives particulars of the trade in the ſhell carried on between Zanzibar, where they are of comparatively little value, and the Weſt Coaſt, where they are uſed as currency.

(P. 117) "Magnice and Cuama Rivers."—Santos, the Portugueſe miſſionary, ſays,—"This River Cuama, which is ſo celebrated, and alſo boaſted of for its riches, is called Zambeſi by the Kaffirs. It riſes ſo far inland that its origin is unknown. The Kaffirs relate that they learn from their anceſtors that this river takes its riſe in a large lake in the middle of Ethiopia, from whence iſſue other large rivers, which flow in various directions, each with a different name; and that in the middle of this lake there are a great many iſlands, peopled by Kaffirs, which are fertile, and abound in game. This river is called Zambeſi, because, on iſſuing from the lake, it paſſes by a large Kaffir town of the ſame name."

I had the opportunity of ſhowing the Copy of Pigafetta to Dr. Holub, whoſe travels to the South of the Zambeſi are well known. He expreſſed his intereſt at ſeeing in this old map the two rivers with which he is ſo familiar—the Limpopo and the Zambeſi, laid down under the names of Magnice and Cuama. Of the tranſition from Magnice to Limpopo we have no information.—*Tr.*

(P. 43) "Mani-Congo."—C'eſt par erreur que l'on dit et que l'on écrit *Mani-Congo*. La dénomination véritable eſt *Muéne-Congo* et par abréviation *Ne Congo*. Ces mots ſignifient "principal maître, principal propriétaire de la terre" (*Muene ixi* ou *Muéne xi*: quelque propriétaire de la terre). Sur preſque toutes les cartes modernes on voit encore la ville du Congo ou de *S. Salvador* (*Saint Sauveur*) portant la déſignation de *Ambassi* ou *Ambassa*, comme nom indigène. C'eſt une erreur qui vient des mots M. Bazi-áncanu, dans le langage du Congo et *M. Bagi-á-mucanu* dans celui d'Angola (Ngola), ou plus proprement de M. Bazi dans le premier et M. Bagi dans le ſecond, et qui ſignifie lieu ou place où le roi du Congo donne audience et rend juſtice.—*Vid. Obs. de J. V. Carneiro; Ann. do. Cons. Ultr.* 1861.

(P. 71) "Messa."—A town on the Atlantic Coaſt of Morocco, midway between Mogadore and Cape Non.

(P. 124) "Monemugi."—Sans vouloir diſcuter l'identification établie par Burton et généralement acceptée, du *Momomugi*, *Munimugi*, ou *Monemugi*, d'alors avec le Ounyamoeſi ou *Unyanuézi* actuel, ce qui en tout cas ne répréſente pas une identification abſolue et qui ſe ſoit conſervée ſans modification par rapports aux limites, nous ferons obſerver que Lopes (comme les autres géographes portugais du XVIe ſiècle) le place déjà au S. de l'Equateur et de ſon *Colve*, entre ſon Lualaba ou ſon Lualaba-Nil et la côte de Quiloa, Melinde et Mombaça. Si l'on admet que ce *Mœnemugi* du XVIe ſiècle eſt réellement *l'Unyamuezi* de notre temps, ſa place ſur la carte de Lopes ne contraire pas entièrement la ſituation qui lui eſt aſſignée de nos jours, et nous ne pourrons établir que cette ſituation, ou plutôt la contrée de *l'Unyamuezi* d'aujourd'hui, ſoit exactement le même qu'elle était au temps de Lopes, ou qu'il le croyait :—la confrontation de ſes calculs avec les révélations des voyageurs modernes à ce ſujet ſemblent ſ'oppoſer à cette extraordinaire ſtabilité de limites et d'étendue d'un état africain. Depuis, c'eſt préciſement au grand lac centrale de Lopes qu'on remarque, d'après ſa deſcription, des individus ſemblables aux Européens, et c'eſt la région de Tanganyika que les marchands arabes ont dès longtemps exploitée. Quant aux richeſſes métallurgiques, *Lopes* les indique partout, et les voyageurs modernes les dénoncent également du côté du *Bemba*. Ce que je crois, d'accord avec Major (Proceed. of R.G.S., June, 1867), c'eſt que le lac de Lopes, correspondant au *U-Kerëué* (lac Victoria) eſt ſon *Colves* (*Kolvé*), placé ſur l'équateur. Le *Bracina* (Barcena, de Barros et d'autres) correſpond évidemment au *Bahr-Tsana* ou Dambia. L'autre lac au N.O. du Colve, et près duquel on lit le nom *Abiami*, peut correſpondre au Muvatan d'où ſort le *Abiad*, et le *Saraboe* eſt très probablement le *Sobat*, malgré une certaine confuſion d'éléments hydrographiques, comme le *Tacazii* de Barros eſt ſans doute le Tacazze ou *l'Atbara* des Arabes. L'hypothèſe que le lac au N.O. pourrait être une modeſte indication du *Muvtan* (lac Albert) ſerait-elle trop audacieuſe? Ce qui me ſemble inconteſtable c'eſt que l'on ne doit point dédaigner cette ſituation des lacs, et que la carte du célèbre explorateur portugais eſt réellement fort remarquable. Et l'on remarquera l'inſiſtence de ces informations et de ces cartes à déſigner un grand région lacuste au centre du grand continent, et à placer les ſources du Nil dans quelques . . . *nyansas*, c'eſt-à-dire, dans quelques "lacs grands comme des mers" (*Alvares*, 1520, 1540), ou dans quelques lacs que les indigènes nomment des mers (*Barros*, *Lopes*, &c., 1552—1591).—*M. L. Cordeiro*, pp. 31, 63—65.

(P. 116) "MONOMOTAPA."—Monomotapa and its "Emperor" are referred to by Livingſtone and Macqueen (ſee *R. G. S. J.* xxvii. pages 112, 117; xxvii. pages 383, 384; and xxx. page 154). The older Portuguefe applied the name Monomotapa to the whole extent of country lying behind the fea-board of Mozambique. The derivation is from Mwene, a lord, and Mutapa, the name of the chief district. The modern name is Chedima. See *Burton's Lands of Cazembe*, page 22, note; and Gamitto and Monteiro, who give an account of Monomotapa, *Davis's Voyages* (Hak. Soc. 1880), page 130, note.

The modern Kingdom of Umzila is alfo regarded as a portion of the Kingdom of Monomotapa.

Fifty or fixty years ago, a Zulu chief, named 'Cnaba, croffed the Limpopo River, conquered the natives up to the Zambefi, and eftablifhed his capital in the falubrious highlands a hundred miles from the coaft. Not long after, he was in turn overthrown by Manikufa, one of the generals of "the great Napoleon of the Zulu fupremacy." The prefent ruler, Umzila, is the fon of Manikufa, and reigns with the defpotic fway of the Kaffir kings. In modern times, this province has hardly been vifited by Europeans. In 1871, Carl Mauch entered it from the weft. The fame year, St. Vincent Erfkine, an envoy of the Colonial Government, vifited Umzila, at his invitation, and fubfequently made three journeys to the king, which made him better acquainted with the country than any other European. From him we learn that the S.W. frontier of the Zulu chief Umzila is now at the commencement of Manhlin, in 22° 50′ S. How numerous the Zulus proper are in Umzila's kingdom is not known. Along the fouth bank of the Zambefi they are not in very good odour. Umzila, however, is paramount ruler of the region in South-Eaft Africa, which has for its northern boundary the lower Zambefi River, and for its fouthern the Uncomafi, or St. George's River, which empties into the Indian Ocean at Delagoa Bay. The coaft-line exceeds 600 miles in length.—*Tr.*

(P. 68) "MUSES OF EGYPT."—Mufa, a genus of plants, the type of the natural order of the *Musaceæ*. This genus is one of the moft important of thofe found in tropical countries, to which the fpecies are confined in a wild ftate. The *Musa Sapientum*, or Plaintain, of which the Banana is a flight variety, has a fruit ufed to a prodigious extent by the inhabitants of the Torrid Zone. The Banana of hot countries is called by botanifts, *Musa Paradisaica*, in allufion to an old notion that it was the Forbidden Fruit of Scripture; it has alfo been fuppofed to be what was intended by the grapes, one bunch of which was borne upon a pole between two men, that the fpies of Mofes brought out of the Promifed Land. The only argument in fupport of the latter opinion is, that there is no other fruit to which the weight of the fruit of Scripture will apply. All the genus is Aſiatic.—*Knight's Cyclo. Nat. Hist.* vol. iii. p. 967.

(P. 111) MUSICAL INSTRUMENTS. The muſical inſtruments now uſed by the Congoeſe are ſuch as the Portugueſe have introduced, ſuch as the trumpet, cornet, French horn, and fife; but the common people are contented with their fifes and tabors at their weddings and other rejoicings. They have alſo ſtringed inſtruments, which, by their rude conſtruction ſeem to be natives of the country; ſuch are their "nſambi" reſembling the Spaniſh guitar, and the "marimba," conſiſting of fifteen or ſixteen ſmall calabaſhes of different ſizes faſtened to a flat board by ſtrings that paſs acroſs their mouths, and which being touched by ſmall pieces of wood, like the ſticks of our dulcimers, yield an agreeable variety of ſounds. Their drums are made of a long hollow trunk of a tree, with a ſingle ſkin ſtretched over one end of it, the other being left open. They are beat either with the fiſts, or by ſticks of heavy wood, and are uſed at their feſtivals, as well as in the army. They are called "ngambo," or "mgombo," and give but a dull, heavy ſound, which is raiſed by that of the fife, or the "longa," which conſiſts of two or more ſmall bells.—*Rees' Cyclo.* vol. ix. It is interesting to notice that a ſimilar name is uſed for the drum among the Waganda people, viz., the "ngomba."—*Tr.*

(P. 116) "NILE SYSTEM."—*João de Barros*, le célèbre hiſtorien portugais du XVIe ſiècle ébauchait rapidement et incidemment de la manière ſuivante dans ſon *Asie*, l'hydrographie africaine :

"Toute le pays que nous avons déſigné ſous le nom de royaume de *Sofala* eſt une grande contrée gouvernée par un principe idolâtre appelé *Benomotapa.*

Cette contrée eſt ceinte comme une île par les deux bras d'un fleuve *qui sort du lac le plus considérable* qu'il y ait dans toute l'Afrique, *lac que les anciens auteurs désiraient beaucoup connaître* comme étant la tête myſtérieuſe *du célèbre Nil et d'où sort également le Zaire* qui coule à travers le royaume de Congo. Et parquoi nous pouvons dire que ce grande lac eſt plus voiſin de notre mer occidentale que de la mer orientale ſuivant la ſituation (long., etc.) de Ptolomée, car de ce même royaume du Congo débouchent dans ce fleuve ſix rivières: Bancare, Gamba, Luylu, Bibi, Mariamaria et Zanculo, qui ſont des fleuves fort abondants en eaux, ſans compter d'autres fleuves ſans nom qui en font *presque une mer navigable* pour de nombreufes embarcations. Dans ce lac il y a des îles d'où fortent des hommes en nombre de plus de trente mille et qui viennent combattre ceux de la terre ferme. Et de ces trois grands fleuves qui, *dit-on présentement*, proviennent de ce lac et qui viennent déboucher dans la mer à une fi grande diftance les uns des autres, celui dont le cours eft le plus étendu *est le Nil que les Abyssiniens du Preste-Joam* nomment *Tacuij et qui reçoit deux autres fleuves remarquables* appelés par Ptolomée *Astabora et Astapus et par les naturels Tacazii et Abanhi* (ce qui fuivant eux ou parmi eux veut dire père des eaux, à caufe de la grande quantité d'eaux que ce fleuve contient). Quoique ce fleuve vienne d'un grand lac nommé *Barcena*, et *Coloa* par Ptolomée, et qu'il contienne des îles, *il n'a rien de commun avec notre grand lac, car d'après les renseignements* que nous avons *au moyen du Congo et de Sofala* ce dernier a plus de cent lieues de longueur. Le fleuve qui descend dans la direction de Sofala, après être forti de ce lac parcourt une grande étendue et fe partage en deux bras dont l'un vient déboucher endeça du Cap des *Correntes;* ce bras eft le même que les nôtres ont *anciennement* appelés fleuve de *Lagoa* et appellent *maintenant Espirito Santo*, nom qui lui a été donné par Lourenço Marques qui eft allé l'explorer en l'année quarante cinq. L'autre bras débouche au deffous de Sofala vingt cinq lieues et eft appelé *Cuama* quoique vers l'intérieur d'autres peuples lui donnent ce nom de *Zambere*." L'erreur de Barros, en 1552, correfpond à celle d'Erhardt en 1856, reproduite encore fur quelques cartes françaifes en 1860. L'un réunit les origines fluviales dans un grand lac, l'autre confond enfemble les lacs Ukereue, Tanganyika et Nyaffa dans une immenfe mer intérieure.—*L. Cordeiro*, p. 43.

The Portuguefe miffionary, Santos, has the following curious theory regarding the Nile:—"Into this kingdom" (of Bagamidri, which he makes ftretch from the equator northwards), he says, "the Nile flows, which takes its rife in a great lake, called *Barcena*, in a defert of Ethiopia, *lat.* 12° *S.* (*according to the most correct information I can gather*). The lake is furrounded by high and fteep mountains, particularly towards the eaft, from whence this river flows, and which is the country inhabited by pagan Kaffirs, called Cafates, who are very powerful favages, and much given to hunting wild beafts. From thence this river flows north-eaft *as far as the second* lake, fituated under the equator, and going ftill further eaft and north-eaft, after croffing fome of the kingdoms of Prefter John, it reaches the Ifland of Meroe, from whence it flows towards the north-eaſt as far as the kingdom of Dambia, which is peopled by Abyſſinian Chriſtians. In this kingdom the Nile forms *a large lake*, 30 *miles long, and* 20 *miles wide.*

(P. 130) "NILE FOUNTAINS."—"Cæterum priores affirmant Nilum maximo impetu ex montibus præcipitem ni subterraneos meatus ferri, eoſque fontes efficere. Utraque harum opinionum falſa eſt: neque enim quiſquam vidit unde Nilus trahat originem."—*Leonis Africani de Africæ descrip.*, Lugd. Bat., 1632, 16mo, pt. ii., p. 742.

(P. 3) "PIGAFETTA."—Our author was in the ſuite of the Legate Caetano, who played an important part during the ſiege of Paris in 1590; and it was in that poſition he remained in that city during the whole time of the ſiege. *De Thou* ("*Memoires de la Société de l'Histoire de Paris et de L'Ile de France.*"—Liv. 99, page 190) thus refers to him:—"Il y avait alors dans Paris un homme connu par ſes longs voyages, nommé Philippe Pigafetta. Il était venu avec le Cardinal Caëtan, et, quelques années auparavant, Philippe II. l'avait déjà envoyé en Angleterre pour reconnaître les côtes et les ports de ce royaume. Nous avons les memoires qu'il publia depuis à ce ſujet. Cet auteur qui eut lui-même beaucoup à ſouffrir pendant ce ſiége, nous a laiſſé pluſieurs traits de la miſère extrême où les Pariſiennes furent alors réduits. P. Pigafetta était le parent, peut-être même le fils (car les dates ſemblent autoriſer cette conjecture) d'Antonio Pigafetta, qui fit le tour du monde avec Magellan (1519—1522). Les biographes nous apprennent que Philippe Pigafetta naquit à Vicence en 1533, et qu'il mourut dans cette même ville le 24 Octobre, 1603. Il ſe diſtingua d'abord comme ingénieur militaire, et pluſieurs des villes du nord de l'Italie lui doivent leurs fortifications. Il parcourut enſuite le Levant, et revint à Malte oû il fut reçu Chevalier, de l'ordre de Saint Jean de Jeruſalem. Sixte Quint, dans le but de former une ligue contre les Turcs, l'envoya en miſſion tantôt d'abord en Perſe, puis auprès de différente cours d'Europe. Il fut Ambaſſadeur, tantôt guerrier, car les mêmes biographes nous diſent encore, qu'il combattu en Croatie, en Hongrie, en Pologne, et ſur différents points de la Méditerranée. Lui-même nous apprend qu'il fit la guerre dans Abruzzes en 1557, et qu'il connut Biron au ſiége de Civitelle où échoua François de Guiſe. En 1591 le Pape, Innocent IX., le nomma ſon camerier, et Ferdinand Ier de Medicis, grand duc de Toſcane, en fit ſon conſeiller intime. Comme Écrivain, Pigafetta a laiſſé pluſieurs ouvrages. Il a écrit un diſcours ſur l'hiſtoire et l'uſage de la bouſſole, paru à Rome en 1586, et un opuſcule relatif à la fameuſe armade Eſpagnole. Mais ſon ouvrage le plus conſidérable eſt certainement la traduction Italienne du traité de tactique de l'Empereur Grec Léon VI. le Philoſophe. Il fit auſſi paraître vers 1600, la traduction de la '*Roma illustrata,*' de Juſte Lipſe, et celle du *Theatre d'Ortelius.* Sa correſpondance avec J. A. Cornaro (1574—1603), eſt à la Bibliothèque Royale de Berlin, Il a laiſſé en manuſcrit une hiſtoire de Vicence."

(P. 20) "PORCELLETTE."—The Portugueſe traveller, Fernão Mendes Pinto, in his travels, calls theſe Porcellette, Porcellana, which is a ſpecies of univalve ſhell.—Cap. 55, v. 65.

(P. 128) "PRESTER JOHN."—This mythical perſonage is aſſigned by ſome writers to Aſia, and by others to Africa. According to the hiſtorian, Moſheim, the firſt account of this potentate is to be found in Abulpharajius, on the authority of a letter from Ebed Jeſu, the Metropolitan of Maru, to the Neſtorian Patriarch, John, in which he deſcribes the converſion of the king of the Tartar people, called Berit, who was baptized by the name John. The chiefs of this tribe ſeem to have joined the prieſthood with their kingly office, and to have gradually extended their ſway. The people over whom they ruled came to be known as the Ung people, and at laſt one of the chiefs was created Ung Khan by the Emperor of China. In the time of this khan began the ſtrife, ſo long waged between the Romaniſts and Neſtorians in Tartary; and in the year 1177, Pope Alexander III. ſent a medical miſſionary, Biſhop Philip, with a letter, which has come down to us, to this chief. No trace of the reſults of this miſſion, however, can be found. In 1202, the rule of theſe prieſtly khans was overthrown by the great conqueror, Jingis Khan, who married the daughter of the laſt khan.

Colonel Yule ſays, "The idea that a Chriſtian potentate of enormous wealth and power, and bearing this title, ruled over vaſt tracts in the far Eaſt, was univerſal in Europe from the middle of the 12th to the end of the 13th century; after which time the Aſiatic glory ſeems gradually to have died away, whilſt the Royal Preſbyter was aſſigned to a locus in Abyſſinia, the equivocal application of the term *India* facilitating this tranſfer. Indeed, I had a ſuſpicion, contrary to the view now generally taken, that the term may from the firſt have belonged to the Abyſſinian Prince, though circumſtances led to its being applied in another quarter for a time. The firſt notice of a conquering

Aſiatic potentate, ſo ſtyled, had been brought to Europe by the Syrian Biſhop of Gabala (*Jibal*, ſouth of Laodicea, in Northern Syria), who came, in 1145, to lay various grievances before Pope Eugene III. He reported that not long before, a certain John, inhabiting the extreme Eaſt, king and Neſtorian prieſt, and claiming deſcent from the three wiſe kings, had made war on the Samiara kings of the Medes and Perſians, and had taken Ecbatana, their capital. He was then proceeding to the deliverance of Jeruſalem, but was stopped by the Tigris, which he could not croſs, and compelled, by diſeaſe in his hoſt, to retire."—*Marco Polo*, V. I., cxlvi. p. 205.

In Mr. Arber's reprint of "Edward Webbe, Chief Maſter Gunner, his Travailes, 1590," we find the following account of Webbe's perſonal experience of Preſter John's Court. The narration does not impreſs one with the idea of Maſter Webbe's truthfulneſs, but rather ſuggeſts that, if a maſter gunner, he was alſo a maſter of the long bow, yet the narrative bears witneſs to the fact that at that time it was the faſhion for travellers to know ſomething perſonally of the mythical Preſter John.

"From Damaſco we went into the land of preſter John who is a Chriſtian, and is called *Christien de Sentour*: that is, the Chriſtian of the Gerdell; againſt this preſter John, I went with the Turks' power, and was then their maiſter Gunner in the field, ye number of Turkiſh Souldiers ſent thither, was five hundred thouſand men who went thither by land, and pitched themſelves in battaile ray at Saran, neere to the place wher the ſon of preſter John keepeth his Court. There Preſter John with his power, ſlew of ye Turks the number of 60 thouſand onely by policie of drawe bridges to let foorth water, made as ſecret ſlewſes for that purpoſe, in which water ſo many Turks periſhed. The next day following, the Turkes' power did incompaſse Preſter John's ſonne and tooke him priſoner, and ſent him for a preſent to ye great Turks' Court then being at Conſtantinople, but ſoone after, preſter John himſelfe made an agreement betweene the greate Turk and his ſonne, that the one ſhould not demand tribute of the other, and ſo his ſonne was releaſed and ſent home againe.

"This Preſter John of whom I ſpake before, is a king of great power, and keepeth a very bountifull Court, after the manner of that Cuntrey, and hath every day to ſerve him at his Table, sixty kinges, wearing leaden Crownes on their heads, and thoſe ſerve in the meat unto Preſter John's Table: and continually the firſt diſh of meat ſet uppon his Table, is a dead man's ſcull cleane picked and laide in black Earth:

putting him in minde that he is but Earth, and that he muſt die, and ſhal become Earth againe.

"I have ſeen in a place like a Park adioyning unto preſter John's Court, three ſcore and ſeventeene Unicornes and Eliphants all alive at one time, and they were ſo tame that I have played with them as one would play with young Lambes.

"When Preſter John is ſerved at his Table, there is no ſalt at all ſet one in any ſalt ſellar as in other places, but a loafe of Bread is cut croſſe, and then two knives are layde a croſſe upon the loafe, and ſome ſalt put upon the blades of the knives and no more."

Mr. Arber, in a Note on Preſter John, after citing the "Encyclopædia Britannica," gives the following intereſting information :—

"Among the curious deſcriptions of this fabulous empire is a ſmall work, printed in French at Rouen in 1506, of which the title is ſimply 'Perreſter Iehan,' while the imprint runs thus: *Cy finent la diversitie des hommes, des bestes et des oiseaux qui sont en la terre de prestre Iehan, Imprimées a Rouen Pour Richard rogerie demourant a Morletz.* It purports to be a letter from Preſter John himſelf to the Emperor of Rome and the King of France, and is dated "from our holy palace, in the year of our birth 506." It is a tiſſue of marvel after marvel: ſo as to render it hardly credible that it was ever ſeriously believed in. A few ſentences will ſhow its character.

"'Preſter John, by the grace of God all powerful king of all the Chriſtians: to the Emperor of Rome and to the King of France, our friends, greeting. We wiſh you to know of our ſtate and of government, that is to ſay, of our people and the different kind of our animals. And becauſe you ſay that our people do not agree in worſhipping God as you do in your country, we wiſh you to know that we adore and believe in the Father, the Son, and the Holy Spirit, who are three perſons in one Deity, and one God alone. And we certify and ſend to you by our letters ſealed with our ſeal concerning the State and manner of our land and of our people. And if you will come into our country, for the good that we have heard of you, we will make you lord after us, and will give you large lands and lordſhips.

"'Know then that we have the higheſt crown in all the world. Alſo gold, ſilver, and precious ſtones, and cities, caſtles, and towns. Know alſo that we have in our country forty-two kings, all powerful and good Chriſtians. Know alſo that we ſupport with our alms all the poor in our land, whether native or foreign, for the love and honour of Jeſus

Chrift. Know alfo that we have promifed in good faith to conquer the Sepulchre of our Lord Jefus Chrift and alfo all the Land of Promife.' "

Sir John Mandevile, knight, tells us (*Voyages and Travels*, &c., London, 1670) that the "Emperor Prefter John is chriftened, and a great part of his land alfo . . . they believe well in the Father, the Son, and the Holy Ghoft. . . . The Emperor Prefter John, when he goeth to Battel, hath no banner borne before him, but he hath borne before him three Croffes of fine Gold, large and great, and richly fet with precious ftones . . . and when he hath no battel, but rideth to take the air, then hath he borne before him but a crofs of a tree. . . . Prefter lived in a city called Suse."

Profeffor Bruun identifies the myfterious perfonage known as Prefter John with Prince Ivanè, of the house of Orpeliani. He was of the royal race of Djenefdan, the chiefs of a Turanian people from that part of Afia which lies between China and the Oural, and, in 1123, delivered the country from Tiflis to Ani out of the hands of the infidels. He died in 1145. According to Profeffor Bruun, another Ivanè, who overthrew Sokman II. in a great battle near Ani, in 1161, was the fame Prefter John who correfponded with feveral potentates in Europe, and the receiver of the letter addreffed by Pope Alexander III. in 1177. In the chronicles of Ibn-Alathir, it is recorded that in the year 1155-56 (a date, however, that does not accord with that given in the Armenian chronicles) the city of Ani was taken from the Emir Cheddad, *by the priests of Armenia.* In the Ivanè called *Juanus rex Georgianorum*, Bruun fees the Prefter John of 1219, who wrote to the Pontiff, Honorius III. In 1247, another Prefter John appears, viz., Taïyang Khan. The Prince George of Marco Polo, and of Giovanni de Montecorvino, was a defcendant of Taiyang Khan.

The ftrife between the Romanifts and the Neftorians caufed the latter to be regarded as unbelievers, and all intereft in them feems to have died out in the weftern world. Then arofe the idea that the traditional king-prieft was to be found in Africa. The firft reports which were brought to Europe of the exiftence in Africa of the fabulous Prefter John came from the Weft Coaft to Portugal. Mr. Major, in "Prince Henry the Navigator," p. 337, gives an account of a great monarch living fome 350 leagues eaft of Benin, the fearch for whofe kingdom, in 1487, made by command of the King of Portugal, led to the great difcovery of the route to India.

Profeffor Zarncke, in his *Abhandlungen der Philologisch-Historischen*

Classe der Königlich Sächsischen Gesellschaft der Wissenschaften, Leipzig: bei S. Hirzel, 1879, regards Yeliulinya as the founder of the Karakhataian Empire in Turkeſtan, and as the real victor over the Sultan Sandjar, in 1141, and, conſequently, as the actual Preſter John, But, inaſmuch as Chineſe hiſtorians repreſent Yeliulinya as a Pagan. and Zarncke himſelf is compelled, whilſt not denying the poſſibility of Yeliulinya having been baptized by the Neſtorians, to aſcribe his fame as a Chriſtian and a prieſt, to the unfounded hopes and lively imagination of the Chriſtians, whoſe diſappointed hopes aſſumed the garb of a myth; it does not appear that Zarncke has thrown further light on the hiſtorical truth of Preſter John than have earlier writers.—*Tr.*

It is intereſting to notice that all the traditions as to the exiſtence of a Chriſtian potentate in the interior of Aſia connect themſelves with the ſpread of Chriſtianity under the Armenians, and the extent of their enterpriſe in this direction is ſhown by the well-known ſtone, which is ſtill in exiſtence, to the north of the Wall of China. It is not impossible that the legends reſpecting Preſter John, and the ſtory of his letters to the Pope and European kings, may be merely mediæval repetitions of the patriſtic traditions regarding King Abgar of Edeſſa, and his letter to our Lord, and ſubſequent letters to the Emperor Tiberius, and to the Kings of Aſſyria and Perſia.—*See Tr. of Syriac Documents acquired by British Museum from the Nitrian Monastery in Lower Egypt, by Rev. B. P. Pratten*, pub. by *T. Clarke, Edinburgh.—Tr.*

(P. 127) "PRESTER JOHN, EMPIRE OF."—The following extracts from Cordeiro's work I have introduced, not ſo much in connexion with the kingdom of Preſter John as for the purpoſe of throwing light on the map compiled by Pigafetta.—*Tr.*

Il ne faut pas toutefois exagérer outre meſure l'erreur attribuée aux géographes du XVIe ſiècle pour ce qui a trait à l'etendue qu'ils donnent à l'empire du *Prestés-João*, et ne pas trop nous préoccuper des limites plus ou moins bien déterminées de l'Abyſſinie actuelle. Voyons qu'elle était l'etendue aſſignée, au XVIe ſiècle et même plus tard, au fameux empire: Longtemps après (Lopes) Jérôme Lobo (*A Short Relation of the River Nile, of its Source and Current* (*Trans.*), London, 1798) faiſait cette remarque:

"This Empire (of Preſter John) anciently commanded many kingdoms and provinces; its own annals and ſome hiſtorians count above twenty, with almoſt as many provinces. What at preſent paſſeth for current is that its greatneſs was notorious, though now limited to five kingdoms, each about the ſize of Portugal, and to ſix provinces, every one differing little from Beyra or Alemtejo."

Voyons quels étaient les pays et royaumes limitrophes du *Prestes-João*, au dire d'Alvares (Franciſco Alvares, Chapelain du roi et natif de Coimbra, partit pour l'Abyſſinie en 1520 avec l'Ambaſſade de *Dom Rodrigo de Lima*), et à ſon époque :

"On the coaſt of the Red Sea and towards the ſouth is a paſtoral people, who move in tribes (*alarves*) of from 30 to 40 families; farther ſtill is the Mooriſh Kingdom (ſic) of *Dangalli*, and next it that of *Adel*, which belongs to Zeilah and Berberah, and extends to Cape Guardafuy, and borders on the kingdoms of Fatigar (Harrah) and Xoa (Choa), which belong to *Prester John.* Next to Adel is the kingdom of Adea (*aduch?*), which is peopled by Moors, and reaches to *Mogadoxo.* To the weſt of the kingdom of Adea are the pagan kingdoms, of which the two firſt, very large ones, are *Gause* and *Gamu.* To the ſouth-weſt of this laſt lies the kingdom of *Gorage.* Still farther weſt is a very large province which forms the kingdom of *Damute*, and in it is the principal ſlave-market. Weſt of this, bordering on a part of the kingdom of Xoa, are the territories of the *Cafates. Now passing from the south and going westwards*," adds Alvarez, "another kingdom belonging to *Prester John* appears, called *Goyame.* This kingdom borders on the Cafates on one ſide, and towards the north on the kingdom of Bagamidri." Alvares did not know its boundaries on the other ſide (W.?); "but it is ſaid," he again aſſerts, "that they are barren mountains." Alvarez alſo writes, "And they ſay that in this kingdom (of Goyame, which, as we have ſeen, he places towards the weſt, or rather ſouth-weſt) riſes, *or flows*, the River Nile, *which is called in this region Gion* (and not Abagni, it muſt be obſerved, a correſponding term in Caſtanhoſo, Barros, &c.), and that *lakes as large as seas are found there.* And in the Kingdom of *Damute*, it is ſaid, riſes a great river contrary to the Nile, for each flows in an oppoſite direction, *but it is supposed this flows to Mani Congo.*"—*Verdadera*, inf. Ed. 1549, C. 129.

Cette dénomination de *Gion* correſpond à l'hypothèſe ſacro-érudite du Géon, Gehon, *fluvius Gion*, ſous laquelle, déjà ſur la carte du Coſmas l'Indico-pleuſtes (VIᵉ ſiècle) paraît le Nil venant du Paradis terreſtre, et qui ſe retrouve encore ſur la carte de Leardus (1448)? C'est poſſible. Mais Alvares l'enregiſtre à peine comme une dénomination locale ou indigène et nous trouvons le terme: *gion* (portugais gião) avec ce dernier caractère dans d'autres écrits ſur l'empire du *Preste*. Lopes dit que le vrai nom de ce souverain eſt *Bel-gian; gian* ſignifiant: prince, &c., et Santos affirme que le côté du Guardafuy à la mer Rouge ſ'appelle *Baragião* (Bahr-el . . . ?). *Duarte Barbosa* (1516) écrit *Barayam* en appellant ainſi la côte de l'Arabie.

Lobo attribue au Abagni l'identidè avec le *Gihon* biblique: "In this territory of Toncua is the *known head and source* of the River Nile by the natives called *Abani*, i. e. the father of the waters, from the great collection it makes in the kingdoms and provinces throughout which it paſſeth . . . This is the river the ſcripture in Gen. ii. calleth Gihon . . ."

Quelques compagnons d'Alvares ſuivirent le *Preste* dans une expédition au royaume d'*Adea* et parvinrent, "prés Mogadàxo." "And they ſay," adds Alvares, "that there is in this kingdom (*Adea*) *a lake as large as a sea, whose shores cannot be seen from it*, and in the lake is an *island*." *Pero da Covilhan* qui était déjà parvenu à cet endroit confirme l'indication qui eſt poſtérieuſement répétée par d'autres écrivains. Le Mogadaxo (Mogadoxo) eſt à peu près placé ſur les cartes modernes comme ſur celle de Lopes (1591) à 2 lat. N. et de ce côté du ſertão on voit ſur les premières, ſeulement le ſuppoſé *Baringo* ou plûtot le *Ukereue*. —*L. Cordeiro*, p. 30–39.

(P. 13) "RAINS, THE."—In his account of the enormous rainfall of Central Africa, and the reaſons he aſſigns for it, we have a remarkable teſtimony to Duarte Lopez's thorough knowledge of the interior of the continent. He is not, however, entirely accurate in the periods he indicates for chief rainfall. Thoſe who wiſh to follow this ſubject ſhould refer to Keith Johnſton's exhauſtive treatiſe in his Handbook on Africa. It is worthy of notice alſo that Pigafetta calls attention to that which all travellers in Central Africa have found ſo trying, viz. the contraſt between the temperature of day and night.—*Tr.*

(P. 130) "RIVER NILE."—La théorie de *Santos* à l'égard du Nil eſt très curieuſe. "Dans ce royaume (de Bagamedri, qu'il étend dès l'équateur vers le N.), dit-il, entre le fleuve du Nil qui nait dans un déſert de l'Ethiopie d'un grand lac nommé *Barzena, situé à* 12° *du côté du Sud* (*d'après les renseignements les plus surs que j'ai pu obtenir*), lac entouré de hautes et abruptes montagnes, ſurtout vers l'E., par où ſort ce fleuve; qui eſt le pays habité par des Cafres idolâtres, nommés Cafates, barbares très robustes et addonnés à la chaſſe des bêtes fauves. De là ce fleuve court au N.E. *jusqu'au second lac qui se trouve sous la ligne*, puis il continue vers l'E. et le N.E. en traverſant quelques royaume du *Preste*, jusqu'à ce qu'il arrive à l'île Meroe, *d'où il se dirige vers le N.E. jusqu'au royaume de Dambia*, peuplé par des chrétiens abyſſiniens. Dans ce royaume le Nil forme *un grand lac qui a* 30 *lieues de longueur* et 20 de largeur."—*L. Cordeiro.*

(P. 7) "St. Helena, Island of."—Captain Cavendiſh, who viſited the Iſland of St. Helena in 1588, confirms the account given by Pigafetta of the diſcovery of the iſland, and of its fertility and productiveneſs.—*Hakluyt*, vol. iii. page 823, edit. 1600.

In the Commentaries of Afonſo Dalboquerque, p. 239, occurs the following intereſting alluſion to the Iſland of St. Helena, where another Lopes is mentioned as being amongſt the renegades who took part in reſiſting an attack upon Beneſtarim, a fortreſs on the mainland, due weſt of the Iſland of Goa :—"This Fernão Lopes, who was the ringleader of the renegades, ſet out on his return to Portugal after the death of Afonſo Dalboquerque, but when he had got ſo far forward on the voyage as the Iſland of Saint Ilena, he made up his mind to ſtay there with a ſlave, who belonged to him, and there he ended his days. He was the firſt who made a habitation in this iſland, eſtabliſhing a hermitage, and planting many trees; and he bred a great number of hogs and goats, ſo that the ſite became a very commodious place of ſhelter for our ſhips which touched there on the homeward voyage from India." *Castanheda*, lib. iii. ch. xciii., and *Correa*, pp. 315, 316, both give information of great intereſt to the political geographer regarding the ſettlement of this man on the Iſland of St. Helena, where, after living for a long time, he died in the year 1546.—*Hakluyt Soc. Edit. of Alboquerque*, 1880, pt. 3, p. 229.

(P. 104) "S. Margherita, Island of."—At Margarita, in the Weſt Indies, was kept the King of Spain's pearl cheſt, and the Earl of Cumberland, in 1598, failed to attack Margarita. Contrary winds, however, prevented the execution of the deſign.—*Athenæ Cantabrigiensis*, vol. ii. p. 418.

(P. 1) "St. Mark, City of."—A ſmall city in N. Calabria—pop. 500, formerly 25,000—ancient name Argentanum. The ſee was founded in 1156; the Biſhop was exempt from the local metropolitan, and ſubject to the Pope only. Antonio Migliori was preſented to the ſee by

Sixtus V., 13th Oct., 1586, but resigned it towards the close of 1591. He was the 34th Bishop.—See *Ughelli, Italia Sacra*, vol. i. page 881.

(P. 10) "SAN THOMÉ, OR ST. THOMAS'S ISLAND."—This is a Portuguese possession, and was first seen by João de Santarem, and Pero de Escobar, two noble Portuguese, who had Fernandez (of Lisbon) and Alvaro Esteves (of Lagos) as pilots. They saw it on December 21st, 1470 (the Feast of St. Thomas).

It was first colonised by João de Pawa, in virtue of a warrant from King João II., dated September 24, 1485, which gave large privileges. One of the chief causes of the subsequent desolation of St. Thomas was the discovery and colonisation of Brazil, the superior climate of which and its vast extent soon attracted all the colonists of St. Thomas. Its chief productions were indigo, sugar, and coffee; and fostered by royal care, this island became the chief emporium of the Portuguese colonial commerce.—*Findlay's S. A. Ocean*, p. 560.

It is one of the five volcanic islands in the Gulf of Guinea, which are evidently a continuation of the volcanic range of the Cameroon Mountains. The highest point on these mountains is 13,000 feet. Next comes the Island of Fernando Po, with its peak 10,190 feet high; next is Prince's Island, a volcanic flower-garden. St. Thomas has a peak 7000 feet high, and a small village, called Santa Anna de Chavas. Last, the little island of Annobon, crossed by bold, rugged basalt masses of wondrous forms, with an extinct crater in the interior of the island filled by a picturesque lake.—*Keith Johnston's Africa.*

Its discovery is thus alluded to by Camoens:—

"The illustrious isle, allied
By name with one who touched the Saviour's side."

Lusiads of *Camoens, canto* v. s. xii.—*Tr.*

(P. 17) "SENO DELLE VACCHE."—South of Catumbella, is Bahia das Vacas, or Santo Antonio, contiguous to which the capital of the kingdom of Benguella has been established.

(P. 1) "SIXTUS V., P."—This Pope was born on the 18th of December, 1521, at Grotto a Mare, near Fermo, and was called Felix Ferretti. The indigent circumstances of his family may be gathered from many little incidents of the child's life; such as his falling into the pond where his aunt was washing, his watching fruit, and even tending swine. Fortunately, there was one member of the family in the

Church, Fra Salvatore, a Francifcan, who, at laft, fuffered himfelf to be prevailed upon to pay the money for his fchooling. When in his twelfth year he entered the Francifcan Order, and retained the name of Felix. Young Felix went to fchool, and carried with him a piece of bread, and at noon sat down and ate it by the fide of a fpring of water, at which he quenched his thirft. Fra Salvatore kept him under very fevere difcipline. Felix often paffed his evenings fafting, and ftudying by the light of a lantern in the crofs-ways, or, if that went out, by the lamp burning before the hoft in the church. We find no record of a marked indication of an innate fpirit of devotion. We learn only that he made rapid progrefs at the fchools and univerfities of Ferrara and Bologna, where he carried off the academic honours with great credit. He won the entire confidence of Pius V., who appointed him Bifhop of St. Agatha, and, in the year 1570, Cardinal. Robed in the purple of the Church, Peretti returned to his native place, as Bifhop of Fermo, where he had once tended cattle. He was elected Pope in 1585. Immediately on ascending the throne he declared his determination of exterminating the banditti and public malefactors, and proceeded to the execution of this arduous work with inflexible refolution. One of his chief fources of gain was the fale of offices. He compelled the juft reviving induftry of the country to minifter indirectly to his advantage. His great advifer in thefe matters was a Portuguefe Jew, named Lopez, who had fled from Portugal from fear of the Inquifition. He had gained the confidence of the datarius, of the Signora Camilla, and, eventually, of the Pope himfelf, who entrusted to him thefe and fimilar operations.—*Ranke's Popes of Rome.*

One of the moft egregious of all literary blunders, is that of the edition of the Vulgate, by Sixtus V. His Holinefs carefully fuperintended every fheet as it paffed through the prefs; and, to the amazement of the world, the work remained without a rival—it fwarmed with errata! A multitude of fcraps were printed to pafte over the erroneous paffages, in order to give the true text. The book makes a whimfical appearance with thefe patches, and the heretics exulted in this demonftration of Papal infallibility! The copies were called in, and violent attempts made to fupprefs it. A few ftill remain for the raptures of the biblical collectors; and at a late fale the Bible of Sixtus V. fetched above 60 guineas—not too much for a mere book of blunders! The world was highly amufed at the bull of the editorial

Pope prefixed to the firſt volume, which excommunicates all printers who, in reprinting the work, ſhould make any alteration in the text !—*Curiosities of Literature*, by I. D'Israeli, p. 30, Ed. 1866. We would, however, refer the reader to the Catalogue of Bibles in the Caxton Exhibition, No. 991.

Sixtus V. is beſt known in Engliſh hiſtory as the Pope who excommunicated Queen Elizabeth, at which ſentence her Majeſty was irreverent enough to laugh, very much to the perplexity of his Holineſs. He died Auguſt 24th, 1590, one year and three months after the final departure of Duarte Lopez from Rome for Congo.—*Tr.*

(P. 51) "We have furnished pictures."—This refers to the original copy, but the pictures are not reproduced in this tranſlation.

(P. 51) "Litter."—The typoya, a deſcription of hammock or ſleeping-net, ſuſpended from bamboos, and which is very comfortable, is ſtill uſed in Angola.

LONDON:
GILBERT AND RIVINGTON, PRINTERS,
ST. JOHN'S SQUARE.

For EU product safety concerns, contact us at Calle de José Abascal, 56–1°,
28003 Madrid, Spain or eugpsr@cambridge.org.

www.ingramcontent.com/pod-product-compliance
Ingram Content Group UK Ltd.
Pitfield, Milton Keynes, MK11 3LW, UK
UKHW012345130625
459647UK00009B/538

* 9 7 8 1 1 0 8 0 8 2 7 4 7 *